MW01241259

THE
MARKETING
GUIDE
FOR
FINANCIAL ADVISORS

**THE COMPLETE REFERENCE FOR
DIGITAL MARKETING, NICHES,
PROSPECTING & POWERFUL IDEAS TO
GROW YOUR BUSINESS**

CLAIRE AKIN, MBA

This book is dedicated to my Dad, who will always be my hero. He has been an Independent Financial Advisor since 1981.

Contents

INTRODUCTION

I'm the type of person that has to believe in the "why" behind what they do every day. Before Simon Sinek spelled out the concept in his book *Start with Why*, I spent a lot of time contemplating the importance of my work and wondering whether I was helping or hurting the world.

During my first job after college, as a buyer for Bumble Bee Foods, I worried about mercury levels in fish and depleting the stock of fish in our oceans. Later, as a medical device marketing rep, I lost sleep over efficacy concerns with the devices I was selling. I actually worked for the Department of Defense for almost a year before I walked away from an interesting and high-paying job. It turns out the Department of Defense is also the Department of Offense, and I didn't want to spend my days buying parts for weapons.

I enjoyed many of the job functions I tried, including sales and working as a financial advisor. But marketing is my passion: it's what I am good at, what I love to do, and what I read about on the weekends for fun. As a marketer, I could probably work in different industries, but I have spent a lot of time thinking through which products I want to help push. Today, as a marketing consultant for independent financial advisors, I've never felt so good about my clients and the value I help them deliver.

Why I Work with Financial Advisors

I grew up in the financial services industry. My dad has worked in the industry for more than 38 years and became an independent advisor as soon as the idea came out in 1981. He has been affiliated with LPL Financial since we called it Linsco Private Ledger and is currently their seventh-longest-tenured advisor. His brother and best friend are also both advisors in the same OSJ, so family gatherings include a lot of investment talk.

As soon as I got my driver's license at sixteen, I started working for my dad's firm after school. Once I got my MBA, I took over his marketing department and worked as an advisor myself. Today I still support his team, but I also work with other advisors to run their marketing. Collaborating with this group of professionals is deeply rewarding and limitlessly fascinating.

Here are a few reasons I work with financial advisors:

1. They're Entrepreneurs

Many of the advisors I work with have similar personalities: they're intelligent, analytical, extroverted, and driven. Could you think of a more interesting group of folks to work with every day? At their core, advisors are entrepreneurs who create and run businesses. This breeds passion, enthusiasm, and fresh ideas to consistently grow. As an entrepreneur myself, I admire the advisors I work with and enjoy learning from and collaborating with them.

2. They Do Important Work

I get frustrated when I hear people talk about advisors as dishonest or greedy. It's unfair that large financial institutions and Wall Street brokers have given everyday advisors a bad rap. Even my personal hero, Tony Robbins, has been bad-mouthing advisors recently, apparently not understanding the difference between brokers and independent advisors.

The advisors I work with spend long hours helping their clients and work even harder to make sure their advice is honest and unbiased. Independent advisors are educators, helping people understand the options available to them so that they can make confident decisions. They help folks save for retirement, create financial security, plan for their children's education, and give to the causes they care about. Our communities and futures are better as a result.

3. They're Members of Our Communities

Growing up with the last name Dobransky and a father who is 6'7" tall, I ran into a lot of people who knew my dad in our town. I can't recall the number of times someone told me what a great guy my dad is, or how he had helped them, or how much they appreciate his work.

When my brother and his friends played Little League, even when times were tight and markets were down, my dad's firm would always pay for the uniforms and team events. I also remember many days when I saw my dad don his black suit and go to a funeral for a client, a neighbor, or a community member.

Advisors are important members of our communities, helping us save for the future and supporting our friends and neighbors. Most advisors I know give back to their communities, whether by raising money for local charities or by educating community members on financial topics. More than any other financial services or professional group, I see advisors giving back to their communities.

4. They're Good People

My first job out of graduate school was in the fast-paced world of medical device sales, touring the country and attending swanky conferences with no FINRA limits on non-cash compensation. On more than one occasion, I saw a sales rep slip off their wedding band as they entered a conference cocktail party, which was disheartening, to say the least.

Despite the reputation that our industry has for greed and corruption, the advisors I know are the most honest, integrous people you could meet. I love attending broker-dealer conferences and seeing the same advisors year after year with their spouses and children. We're part of a lovely group of people who work hard and do the right thing for their clients and their families.

5. They Help People

During my childhood, I was alarmed a few times when we came home to tearful messages on our answering machine from a client whose spouse had died. At first, I worried that my dad's clients were dying off and there would soon be none left. But over the years, I noticed that he was often the first person they called when tragedy struck.

People list doctors, lawyers, and accountants in the same category as financial advisors in terms of the role they play in their clients' lives. But could you imagine calling your doctor or lawyer to lean on during a divorce or following a death? Client meetings can feel like therapy sessions at times, and some advisors I know are trained in crisis counseling. The role advisors play in their clients' lives is much more than financial.

Last week, I was on the phone with an advisor I work with who was driving home 100 miles after helping an elderly client move into a retirement home. Another advisor was running late to lunch because he had been helping his client shop for a new car. My dad is always accompanying his elderly clients to make big decisions, go to the DMV, or move furniture. Having someone you can call during times of need is an important benefit of working with a trusted advisor.

If you are an advisor, I want to thank you for all you do to serve your clients and your community. I am happy to support you in providing a valuable and significant service. While you work hard and shoulder tremendous responsibility, the skeptics question your integrity and compliance never cuts you a break. It may not be easy, but the work you do sure is important.

WHY I WROTE THIS BOOK

I talk to advisors on the phone every day and a lot of them are frustrated. Marketing strategies that worked in the past don't work anymore. Their clients are getting older and drawing down their assets. They need to grow their business but they have no idea how. Many of them are considering closing up shop unless they can figure out a solution to get more clients.

I wrote this book to share what I know with advisors like you so that you can help more people in your career and find more fulfillment in your life.

Those same advisors ask me every day, "What should I be doing with my marketing?" The truth is that "should" is a relative term. The answer depends on two things:

- What are your marketing goals?
- How much are you willing to put into your marketing?

Similar to attending a conference or working out with a trainer, you can expect to get out what you put into your marketing, as long as you use your resources in an effective way. Because we know what works in marketing for financial advisors today, the outcome is a function of the goals you set and the time and energy you put toward those goals.

If you would like to grow your AUM by 15 percent next year, I recommend investing at least 5–7 percent of your revenue into your marketing budget. However, if your goal is to help support your referral process and double your referrals next year, putting 2–3 percent of your revenue will likely suffice.

Most advisors understand that marketing is important, but many have been burned in the past by marketing "experts" and expensive schemes that did not deliver results.

It's my mission to demystify marketing for advisors and give simple and actionable advice you can trust.

If you're looking to create your ideal marketing plan, here are the six most important building blocks, which we will cover in this book:

1. Build a Brand That Creates Trust

Creating a brand that speaks to your specific niche makes all of your other marketing efforts more effective. Make sure your business name and brand inspire trust. This includes your logo and any brand imagery, which should be professional and consistent.

2. Develop a Website with Horsepower

Advisors need a great website to compete online. But before you get too hung up on design and content, think about function. Your website should be mobile responsive, be secure, have built-in forms that capture leads, include blogging functionality, and have event registration capabilities. This well-built engine will make your marketing more powerful and will save you time and energy in the long run.

One of the biggest marketing mistakes I see is spending months and thousands of dollars on perfecting a new website. When we look at the before-and-after statistics of advisors who have spent more than $10,000 on new sites, there is no more traffic as a result. After your site looks good and functions well, any additional time and money will yield diminishing returns.

3. Improve Your Google Analytics and SEO

Verified business listings show up on Google Maps, include photos and business information, and can be dialed from a mobile phone with one tap. Having a verified business listing improves your website's SEO and helps prospects find you. Registering your business with search engines is the fastest way to improve SEO, and the registration does not need to be updated unless you change your business address.

4. Create Beautiful Email Campaigns and Blog Content

With an email marketing engine, it's easy to create great-looking, mobile-friendly email campaigns that include powerful features such as A/B testing, targeting, automation, and analytics. I recommend MailChimp or Constant Contact.

The bread and butter of an effective marketing plan is quality custom content that your prospects find interesting and valuable. Luckily, you're the natural expert on the financial topics your clients and prospects want to know more about. Turning that expertise into consistent content marketing is where the magic happens. I recommend at least monthly custom articles that go out via email, blog, and social media.

5. Create a Rock-Solid Social Media Presence

Because Google gives preferential treatment to LinkedIn when returning search results, your profile is as likely to come up for a name search as your website. For this reason, your LinkedIn profile (along with all of your social media profiles) should look as great as your website and maintain your branding. Optimize each of your social media profiles for SEO and match them to the look and feel of your website.

6. Use Technology to Get in front of New People

The last 5 years have seen several advances in technology that you can now incorporate into your marketing plan, including webinar, pop-ups, and online appointment schedulers. Embracing these advances will help you gain new clients, retain the ones you have, and build a business that will last.

Before you invest in your marketing, take some time to think through your long-term goals and consider which pieces of the puzzle you already have in place. There are plenty of effective techniques to get more mileage out of content, videos, and publications you have already created.

Fancy websites and marketing materials are only as powerful as the traffic that you drive to them. By building a cohesive marketing framework and reusing existing collaterals, you'll be able to get the most out of your marketing budget.

The Truth about Marketing for Financial Advisors

THE NEXT TIME a marketer tells you that it's easy to get a dozen new leads a week using Facebook ads, ask yourself whether there are hundreds of qualified prospects in your area choosing to work with a financial advisor because they see an ad in their Facebook feed. Unfortunately, that's just not realistic.

Even top advisors have to think long and hard about how to find qualified prospects and spend time and money to create marketing strategies that work. The first step is realizing that choosing a financial advisor is an important decision that people don't (and shouldn't) take lightly.

Every day, I make it a point to spend at least an hour on the phone with independent financial advisors talking about their marketing. We review what they've tried in the past, what has worked, and what was a waste of money. Through these conversations, I have uncovered a fundamental misunderstanding that advisors often share: that marketing should be easy.

Marketing *can* be easy, depending on what you're selling. It's easy to get people to order a cheap new gadget on Amazon. It's easy to get people to sign up for a free webinar. It's even easy to get people to come to a free steak dinner to learn about annuities. But finding qualified prospects who are in a position to hire you now is not that easy.

How Many Qualified Prospects Are There?

Let's say that as an independent financial advisor, you're looking for clients in their 50s or 60s who have $500,000 or more in investable assets. While you probably hear all the time that there are ten thousand Baby Boomers retiring every day, that doesn't mean that they're all qualified prospects.

Many of them have no savings and plenty of debt. According to Money.com, one in three Americans has nothing saved for retirement. Data from a 2013 U.S. Census survey shows that the median nest egg of the 59 percent of 65-year-olds that have saved *anything* for retirement is only about $104,000.

How Often Do People Hire a Financial Advisor?

Choosing someone to manage your money is different from purchasing a handbag or even a car, in that most people only make the decision to hire a trusted financial advisor once in their lifetime. Many people will purchase a house more often than they will hire a financial advisor.

Let's consider that of the small fraction of Baby Boomers who have at least $500,000 in investable assets, over 35 percent are already working with a financial advisor (according to a 2016 Harris Poll).

For the remaining fraction who have saved at least a half a million dollars without a financial advisor, let's think about their buying process. Their obvious decision is to continue to run their finances on their own. Hiring a financial advisor is only a secondary option.

How Do People Choose a Financial Advisor?

There are an estimated 300,000 financial advisors in the United States. We know that most people choose a financial advisor who is near their physical location. They could choose a robo-advisor or hire someone at the Edward Jones office down the street. *So, for the fraction of Baby Boomers with money to invest who are looking for a financial advisor in your area, how do you stand out?*

There's a lot of confusion out there about how independent financial advisors get new clients, and – as I found while I was looking for concrete data for an upcoming webinar I'm creating – not a lot of statistics on the subject. But then I realized that I actually have access to the data I needed!

Each year, we run surveys to help advisors understand what their clients care about the most. One of the questions on our survey is "Why did you decide to work with our firm?" We know the answer to this question is critical for advisors to hone their specialty.

I took a sample of the latest surveys we've run and began organizing the responses into broad groups. I was surprised that every single answer actually fit into one of just six categories. According to our data, here are the main ways people choose an advisor.

How People Really Choose a Financial Advisor

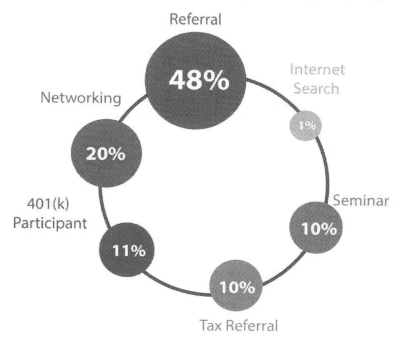

Referral

Almost half of respondents said they chose to work with their advisor because they had been referred to them.

Marketers and business coaches may tell you that top advisors are raking in new clients with radio shows or Facebook ads. But the reality is that with all the technology in the world today, people are still choosing an advisor the same way they always have: by asking for a referral from friends, family, and coworkers they perceive to be successful.

Networking

About 20 percent of people chose their advisor because they had met them at an event or in person – for example, through church, friends, or a cycling group.

401(k) Participants

About 11 percent of clients chose their advisor after working with them through their employer-sponsored 401(k) plan.

Tax Client Conversion

About 10 percent of clients chose to work with an advisor from the firm they used to prepare their taxes. For advisors who offer tax services, this model is a great way to bring on new assets.

Seminar or Event

Another 10 percent of new clients came on board after hearing the advisor speak at a seminar, including one event on college planning and another on alternative investments.

Internet Search

Only one new client had made their decision on the basis of an Internet search. This supports the idea that people do not type "financial advisor" into Google and hand over their life savings.

How to Get More Referrals

What does this mean for advisors trying to grow their business? Referrals have got to be at the core of your marketing strategy. And how do you get more referrals?

- First, you have to be *referable* by embracing a specialty. What one urgent problem do you solve for a specific group?
- Next, you have to stay top-of-mind by reminding people what you do and how you can help them.
- Finally, you must keep letting people know that you're taking on new clients and regularly ask for referrals.

Generating New Leads through a Specialty

I'll be honest here, generating new leads who do not already know you is a really tough challenge. People will not (and should not) give their life savings to a financial advisor they haven't vetted. Too many stories about bad players in the past have left investors skeptical and slow to trust someone who wants to manage their money.

So why would someone invest with you if they were not referred by a person they trust? Because you're a specialist. The only way I see advisors get new leads who are not referrals is by harnessing the power of being a specialist. By positioning yourself as the go-to expert for an urgent problem your prospects are trying to solve, you open the door to non-referral leads.

Embracing a specialty and creating content to address that niche is the best way to get in front of new leads. Take a look at the top five blog posts of the past year for the hundreds of advisors we work with. Three of the five are specialist articles where the advisor is the authority in their field. The other two are foundational pieces to help support the advisor's referral process.

1. "How to Correct an Overfunded Defined Benefit Plan"

    This advisor is a 401(k) specialist and helps business owners create and optimize their retirement plans. This post received more than 2,000 views on the day it went out and thousands of follow-up views via Google searches on the subject.

2. "See a Sample Financial Plan"

    This is a blog post we do for almost all of the advisors we work with because we know it works. One advisor we work with had 1,500 views of this post in the past 3 months alone. We also add a button to the advisors' homepage that visitors can click to see a sample plan. Prospects want to know what they'd be purchasing by working with you, and this is always one of the most visited pages on our advisors' websites.

3. "Could a Deferred Sales Trust Help Reduce Your Tax Bill?"

    For this specialist advisor, a post on the thorny topic of deferred sales trusts got more than 1,100 views the day it went out and hundreds more in the weeks that followed. High-quality, specific content is always a hit.

4. "The Intersection of Life Coaching and Financial Planning"

Creating marketing content is all about showcasing what makes you different. What makes one top advisor we work with unique is that he provides life coaching along with financial planning. His post on the intersection of the two got hundreds of views and shares via social media.

5. "New Tax Bill Approved: Here's What It Means for You"

Timely reactions to current events provide a great opportunity to get in front of clients and prospects. This top-performing blog post was sent out as soon as a new tax bill was approved. The advisor's clients shared it with friends and family, resulting in hundreds of extra views and a few new referrals.

You need to come up with at least one piece of content that gets a lot of views from your ideal prospects and converts them to warm leads. Reading your content (or watching your video) should make them ask questions or want to discuss their specific situation with you.

Finding Your Specialty

Everybody wants to feel special. We don't want to eat in generic restaurants, we don't want to drive boring cars, and we don't want to hire forgettable advisors to invest our money. Clients want to feel like they've found the best-suited advisor for their circumstances. One conversation I have every single day with financial advisors is about embracing a niche through their marketing. The riches are in the niches, I tell them. For marketing to be successful, it needs to be focused. But it's a hard sell.

Whether you specialize in non-profit Christian financial planning, planning for divorcees, or wealth management for dentists who own their practice, owning a niche allows you to know exactly where to find your prospects and to market directly to them. They will feel special in your hands and be much more resistant when approached by generic competition. Clients have friends who are a lot like them, and it's easy for your clients to refer friends to your specialty practice if you are the best in your niche.

How to Embrace a Niche without Alienating Anyone

The most successful advisors I work with have fully embraced one or two laser-focused specialties. Still, most advisors are hesitant to embrace a niche for fear of alienating people who don't belong to that group.

To focus on a specialty without alienating people outside of that group, you can speak to two or three niches on your website. Start with the niche that represents the clients you serve best, such as:

- Business owners preparing to sell their firm to a family member
- Divorcees who want their settlement to last a lifetime
- Recently laid-off Qualcomm executives

Then, create a second, broader segment that includes everyone else you work with, such as:

- Families pursuing financial freedom
- Professionals planning for retirement
- Hard-working people concerned about their financial future

or my personal favorite:

- Nice people who need help with their financial plans

Who doesn't consider themselves part of that group?

By embracing a specific niche as well as a broader counter-niche, you get the best of both worlds. Your network will understand what you do best and can easily refer people who need your help. You will avoid confusing current clients or alienating prospects.

Examples of Successful Dual Niches

Top advisors often embrace three or more niches, some even micro-specific. One advisor I work with serves physicians, but not just any physicians, only those that own their own practice and also need tax planning help.

Here are some real-life examples of dual niches that have performed well for advisors:

- Business owners seeking true wealth and families pursuing financial freedom
- Medical/pharmaceutical reps and pre-retirees
- Female CEOs, LGBT families, and successful business owners

If your marketing feels stagnant, it may be that you're trying to be everything to everyone. For marketing to cut through the noise today (and there's a lot of noise when it comes to financial planning content) it needs to be specific and targeted.

To get started choosing your ideal niche(s), make a list of your ten favorite clients and identify what they have in common. Consider whether you could embrace a specialty serving people just like them or groups who are facing the same financial planning concerns.

Answer the Most Important Marketing Question Ever

Stan Mann, a top coach to financial advisors, poses the most critical marketing question in an inspiring way: *"What one urgent problem do you solve for a specific niche?"* The answer to this question is the heart of your marketing strategy. Have you taken the time to articulate your answer?

Having a one-sentence explanation of the urgent problem you solve for a niche set of clients is critical for your marketing for three reasons:

- First, we need your existing clients to be able to answer that question so they can introduce you to folks who need your help.
- Second, we need referrals to understand your answer so they believe that you're singularly suited to help them.
- Third, we need to communicate your answer to prospects through your marketing to attract your ideal clients.

Do You Have an Answer?

Very few advisors have taken the time to answer this important question. Have you? Maybe you aren't comfortable limiting your scope. Of course you do more than solve one problem for a specific group of people. But for your marketing efforts, it pays to be specific.

In my case, *I help specialist advisors target their ideal prospects with content marketing.* I do other things, such as teach advisors how to use LinkedIn and run search engine optimization for their websites, but the core of my work is content marketing for advisors with a true specialty.

I find that most advisors either draw a blank or give way too much information when asked what they do and who they serve. What about you? Here are a few good examples from advisors I know:

- *We help LGBT executives retire on time.*
- *I help anesthesiologists prepare their practices for a buyout and retire.*
- *We help business owners remove assets from their business so they can find true wealth.*

How to Create Your Answer

I find that it helps to picture your top clients mentioning your firm to their friends. What would you like them to say? How would you like them to position your expertise? Often, clients aren't sure how to introduce you to people in their network who need your help. They may say, "We really trust him" or "She's helped us with our financial plan," but that doesn't convey your expertise or explain why you're the best person to help the referral.

To make an impact, we need them to position you as the go-to expert in your niche. It's important to prime them with a simple statement that explains exactly what you do and how you help. Through your marketing, you should repeat this idea over and over until everyone you know understands and can communicate your particular specialty.

If you don't have a clear, one-sentence answer to the question *"What one urgent problem do you solve for a specific niche?"* take 10 minutes today to come up with one!

Stay Top-of-Mind

To get more referrals, you'll want to send out thoughtful, personalized content on a regular basis to stay top-of-mind. Staying top-of-mind by reminding people what you do and how you can help makes it easy for them to refer you when they come across someone who needs your help. This is content marketing, and you can learn more about it by reading Joe Pulizzi's book *Content, Inc.*

Now is the time to build out your marketing calendar for the year so that it flows naturally. Below is a marketing calendar we recommend to all of our new clients. It includes the top-performing blog posts that we've tested with hundreds of advisors.

Month 1

"Why I Became an Advisor"

The goal of this post is to tell your story and let your network know why you do what you do. This creates a powerful and memorable connection with clients and prospects. The concept comes from Simon Sinek's book *Start with Why*. This is always the most popular post we create for advisors.

Month 2

"What We Do and How We Can Help"

Your clients may know what you've done for them, but they may not be aware of all of your services and what you do best. This post allows them to refer you more easily when they come across someone who needs your help.

Month 3

"See a Sample Financial Plan"

Prospects want to see what they are considering buying before they take the time to meet with you. The "Sample Financial Plan" post is often the most visited page on our advisors' websites.

Month 4

"You Can Now Make an Appointment Online!"

We help our clients get setup with online appointment scheduling technology so prospects can take the next step and schedule a 15-minute phone call with you, twenty-four hours per day!

Month 5

"Please Join Us for Our Client Appreciation Event"

As part of our Referral Marketing Package, we help promote your events by creating registration pages, sending invitation emails, and posting about them on social media.

Month 6

"We're Never Too Busy to Help Someone You Know"

Do your clients know that you're taking on new clients? Many may think you're busy or at capacity. Reminding them that you're available to speak with their friends, family, and coworkers helps generate more referrals.

Month 7

"What to Do during a Market Decline"

It's critical to stay in front of clients during good times and bad, since during market declines, clients tend to think about moving their money. Communicating proactively about market downturns is a great way to get referrals, because clients tend to forward emails like this to their nervous friends and family.

Month 8

"Case Studies: Three Recent Clients We've Helped"

Explaining who you serve, how you help, and the benefits of working with you is a critical foundation of your marketing strategy. We create this post and add it to your homepage.

Month 9

"What's New at Our Firm?"

It's important to update your network at least once a year on happenings at your firm, including fresh team members, new technologies, and events you may be having.

Month 10

"Please Take Our Annual Client Survey"

When was the last time you conducted a client survey? Top advisors do client surveys each year because they know it's the best way to get feedback, identify problems, and ask for referrals.

Month 11

"Our Year-End Economic Update"

Near the holidays is a good time to update your network on the economy and your investment outlook. It's also a great time to remind them that you're taking on new clients as they start the busy season of mingling with friends and family.

Month 12

"Happy Holidays from XYZ Financial Planning"

The holidays are a great time for a personal update. Send out your family photos, let your network know what you're up to, and share what you're most thankful for. Invite clients and prospects to schedule an appointment in January to make updates to their financial plan.

By investing in content marketing, you make it easy for people to forward your emails to their friends, family, and coworkers. We know that the top way people choose a financial advisor is by asking their friends, family, or a coworker for a referral, so this strategy is the key to driving more referrals.

CHAPTER 2

Sharing Your Story through Content Marketing

What Is Content Marketing?

CONTENT MARKETING IS the creation and distribution of content to earn the attention of prospects. Once you have their attention, they get to know you better and take the next step toward working with you. If you want to learn everything there is to know about content marketing, read *Content, Inc.* by Joe Pulizzi, which is a great resource with a host of business examples.

You've likely been the target of content marketing from companies sending you eBooks, whitepapers, podcasts, and more. The goals of content marketing are to:

- Earn the attention of prospects
- Show them what you do and how you can help
- Position yourself as a subject matter expert
- Stay top-of-mind
- Start a conversation
- Drive traffic to your LinkedIn profile or website

The strategy can be effective with general or "canned" content, but it is most effective when the content you create is specialized and original. You may be using a form of content marketing today if you're sending out market commentaries, videos, or other third-party produced content to stay on top of your prospects' mind. However, there has been a backlash against generic content in recent years, as we all tire of the noise.

Have you received an obviously mass-produced health or lifestyle article from your real estate agent or dentist? That type of content is annoying, because if you wanted to learn about the "Top Ten Vacation Spots in Europe," you would Google it yourself. Effective content marketing uses custom, original content that provides value specifically to your target demographic.

Instead of:

"Ten Retirement Planning Mistakes"

Try:

"How to Maximize Your General Electric Benefits Package"

Instead of:

"Three Reasons to Use a Financial Advisor"

Try:

"Why I Became a Wealth Advisor to Single Women"

Instead of:

"Ten Keys to Investing"

Try:

"What Should You Do After Last Week's Stock Market Decline?"

People in your network don't want to be bombarded with generic content, but they are interested in reading your expert opinion and insights on a newsworthy topic. High-quality custom content addresses this need.

Why You Should Create Regular Valuable Content

1. **Blogging may improve your website's search engine optimization,** helping prospects locate you. If you incorporate keywords that your ideal prospects would be searching for, your blog post and website will rank higher.

2. **Blogging allows you to connect with clients on current topics.** It's a great way to keep in touch, answer frequently asked questions, and educate clients and prospects.

3. **Regular posts can help to establish your expertise** as a thought leader in your specific niche.

4. **Your posts give you higher referability** by providing clients with valuable content that they may share with friends and family.

5. **It can be fulfilling to express yourself** and share your knowledge with your network.

Creating Content

Top advisors spend a significant portion of their work hours creating their own custom content. Michael Kitces, who is often ranked as the most social media savvy advisor in the United States, spends a full 20 percent of his week writing for his blog. His content marketing strategy has helped grow his firm, Pinnacle Advisory Group, to more than $1.8 billion in AUM. He is also an author and speaker, and he frequently appears in the media.

However, if you don't have time or don't enjoy creating your own content, it's perfectly okay to outsource the job. Be sure that whoever creates your content keeps true to your opinions, insights, and philosophies. My firm's bread and butter is creating and deploying custom content for top advisors, in the form of blog posts, LinkedIn publications, eBooks, whitepapers, and email marketing. By outsourcing the job, they are able to take marketing off their plate and focus on what they do best.

If you know that you will not create content consistently, skip this section and outsource the task. It's more important to get the job done than to do it yourself. Although I create my own original content each week, I outsource the deployment of it because I don't enjoy the task and know I'm likely to procrastinate.

If you happen to be a proficient writer or speaker, creating your own content can put you way ahead of the competition. Be sure to commit to a schedule (I recommend at least every other week) and put aside time make it happen. And lways bear two key points in mind as you create content:

Be Clear on Your Niche

Who do you serve and how do you help them? Each piece of content should reiterate this point, no matter the subject. Every time someone engages with a piece of content, make sure to remind them that you are the go-to resource for your main thing.

Answer Your Prospects' Most Pressing Questions

Content marketing, in general, is aimed at helping people find you when they need you most. One direct way to do this is to answer the questions they are likely to type into Google. Oftentimes, I work with advisors to create posts that are the only answer available on Google for a common question their clients and prospects ask.

My dad works with researchers and scientists at UC San Diego, where employees have the choice between a 457 and a 403(b) plan. He is commonly asked what the difference is, so we created a blog post titled "What Is the Difference between the UC San Diego 457 and 403(b) Plans?" and another on "Making the Most of Your UC San Diego Employee Benefits." Posts like these are likely to be shared among groups of employees and between your clients and their coworkers, fostering referrals.

Another advisor I work with serves widowed and divorced spouses, so we created a series of posts on "The First Financial Steps to Take When Widowed" and "Five Financial Mistakes Widows Should Avoid." Posts like these are effective in helping prospects who were referred to your website or LinkedIn profile get comfortable with your experience and expertise before they decide to make an appointment.

This marketing approach requires some research upfront. You will need to listen to your current clients and understand their concerns. You may be surprised to find that what you have been talking about is not exactly what they are worrying about.

Make a list of topics that you want to cover and then choose a content vehicle that you think would best communicate each subject. For example, if you want your clients to consider rolling over their IRA accounts, you might find an infographic that shows how many Americans are doing that right now. Or you might find a video that tells the story of a couple who benefited from making the move. You might write an article that details the options available or post a blog about your experience with a client who procrastinated and suffered a few losses as a result. You could even create a list of ten mistakes to avoid when rolling over an IRA.

Key Principles of Marketing Content

As you create and/or curate content, consider the following key principles, which are used by the most successful communicators in every industry. Use these keys to unlock the power of content to strengthen relationships and build your network.

Marketing Content Key #1: Don't Just Share Facts; Tell Stories

Let's face it: Your clients don't care about your marketing goals. But everyone likes a good story! People will be drawn to you as you tell your story through digital media and as you encourage them to share their stories as well. The most successful financial advisors know how to weave stories into their websites, social pages, and presentations. Surprise your digital visitors by sharing a few pictures and brief stories that illustrate a point.

Marketing Content Key #2: Create a Community

One of the hallmarks of inbound marketing is the goal of generating conversations. As you reach out with valuable information, you should always ask for comments and questions and make it easy for people to respond. Speak to the comments you receive in a blog post or online presentation, or by posting content about a comment on your sites. (Say something like, "I received a great question the other day about the future of the Roth IRA. Here is a video that addresses that topic.") You can also use your content platforms to let clients know that you're listening to their concerns and that you have something interesting to share in response.

Marketing Content Key #3: Continue to Build Your Brand

Like it or not, you are a brand. Your business has a certain feel and flavor to it. The design and style of your website should reflect (and even enhance) the feeling clients get when they come into your office. This builds your personal brand. Be consistent in your messaging across all your platforms. Your colors, your photography, your mission statement, and your supporting content should look and feel the same on your website, social pages, and mobile app. This doesn't mean you have to say the same thing everywhere, but it does mean that your clients should be able to recognize your brand wherever they see it.

No matter how you obtain it, all the marketing content you deploy should follow the prime objective of inbound marketing: Address the concerns of potential clients with valuable information. In other words, your content should answer your prospects' most pressing questions. Begin your content creation with an evaluation of your potential clients. Rather than asking yourself, "How can I get my message out to high-net-worth individuals?" consider instead, "What is my target market worrying about right now? What content would best address their biggest financial concerns? What questions are they Googling?"

Marketing Content Key #4: Use a Market Correction to Create Content

How much would you bet that the market will decline 10 percent or more at some point within the next year? I hope you'd bet something, not just because the market has been hovering around all-time highs, but because a 10 percent correction has happened on average about once per year from 1900 to 2018.

Financial advisors know that market declines are a normal part of investing. But if you know that a correction is coming, why not have a marketing campaign ready to take advantage of the event?

Downturns present powerful marketing opportunities for two reasons. First, your marketing campaign about a correction is likely to get twice as many views as other campaigns. Second, prospects have unprecedented urgency to act during an uncomfortable market decline.

✓	Happy Thanksgiving From Nobile Hinchey Private Wealth Management Regular · Michael Nobile Client Newsletter **Sent** on Thu, Nov 26, 2015 7:00 am	**153** Subscribers	**46.6%** Opens	**13.7%** Clicks
✓	What Should You Do After Last Week's Market Decline? Regular · Michael Nobile Client Newsletter **Sent** on Mon, Jan 11, 2016 5:11 pm	**145** Subscribers	**42.1%** Opens	**28.3%** Clicks

John Steinbeck's *East of Eden* offers an interesting observation on water cycles in California that reminds me of the way we all tend to relate to stock market cycles:

> *The water came in a thirty-year cycle. There would be wet and wonderful years when the land would shout with grass. And then the dry years would come. The land cracked and the springs dried up and the cattle listlessly nibbled dry twigs. Some families would sell out for nearly nothing and move away. And it never failed that during the dry years the people forgot about the rich years, and during the wet years they lost all memory of the dry years. It was always that way.*

When the market goes down, you're inundated with phone calls and doing your best to placate nervous clients. There's no time to create and launch a campaign that uses the correction as a marketing opportunity. The good news is that with pullbacks coming about every year, you have an annual marketing opportunity to reach prospects at their peak point of urgency. You could practically build a spot into your marketing calendar for this piece of communication. Now is the time to get a post ready to go that not only reassures your clients but offers a referral opportunity.

Why You Need to Communicate During Volatility

- **Proactive communication is good client service.** Your clients hire you not only to help them plan for their financial future, but to educate them in good times and in bad. They are eager to get an explanation of what's going on and receive some guidance on what they should do about it.

- **It's your job to keep clients from selling when the market is down.** We all know that behavior is an important component of long-term investment success and that when clients are feeling the urge to sell when the market is low, it's your place to remind them of their long-term plan.

- **Proactive communication results in fewer phone calls and panicked clients.** If you're able to act quickly, clients are more likely to trust that you're prepared for the volatility and they'll feel they're in good hands. This results in less time spent educating and calming individual skittish clients.

What Should You Say about a Correction?

I believe that most advisors don't prepare communications in advance of downturns because they know that each event is different and they're waiting to fill in the specifics. However, no matter the cause of the market drop, your key messaging will be the same:

- **This is expected.** Explain that you have been anticipating a downturn and that it's a normal and healthy part of market cycles. Point to historical data that shows the frequency of similar events.

A History of Declines (1949-December 2018)

Type of Decline	Average Frequency[1]	Average Length[2]	Last Occurrence[3]
-5% or more	About 3 times a year	44 days	December 2018
-10% or more	About once a year	114 days	December 2018
-15% or more	About once every 4 years	270 days	December 2018
-20% or more	About once every 7 years	431 days	December 2018

Source: RIMES, Standard & Poor's.

[1] Assumes 50% recovery rate of lost value.

[2] Measures market high to market low.

[3] The average frequency and average length rows exclude the most recent decline in December 2018 because the 50% recovery of lost value occurred after 12/31/18.

- **Your portfolio is not down as much as the market.** Remind your clients that while the S&P 500 may be down 10 percent, their accounts are not invested in the index and have therefore declined less than the market.

- **Now is not the time to sell.** Explain that no one can consistently predict the right time to get in or out of the market. It's human nature to lose patience and sell at or near the bottom of a downturn. Even if you were able to get out early in a decline, you'd still have to guess when to get back into the market – and you'd likely guess wrong.

- **You have not realized any losses yet.** You only realize losses when you sell, so it's critical not to sell when the market is down. It's normal to feel uncomfortable when the market is down, especially if you're approaching retirement. However, each time in history that the market has gone down, it has come back up again. Downturns of 10 percent are likely to return to normal within about 115 days, based on historical data.

- **Stay focused on the long term.** Remind clients that you've built their financial plan and investment strategy for the long term, with short-term volatility accounted for. While a correction can be upsetting, there's no reason to deviate from their long-term financial plan.

- **Call if you have questions.** Encourage them to get in touch if they are feeling nervous or want to review their accounts.

How to Use a Correction to Get Referrals

Now that you've proactively communicated with your existing clients, it's time to use the market downturn as an opportunity. The Red Cross is always at the ready to deploy fundraising campaigns as soon as a disaster strikes. This doesn't make them greedy; it simply allows them to strike while the iron is hot so they have the funds to tackle the disaster.

Downturns bring precious urgency in prospects that we don't find at any other time. In marketing, our arch-nemesis is lack of urgency. Folks who have put off financial planning for most of their lives are not easily pushed into action when times are good. But when times are bad, things get very uncomfortable and they're more willing to talk. Here's how to go after referrals when times are bad:

- **Include a deal for clients' friends and family.** Offer to provide a free second opinion and recommendations to minimize losses.

- **Provide an easy action to take.** Share a link to schedule a 15-minute investment review by phone. This way, even if prospects read your email after hours, they can take action when they're feeling peak urgency and sleep better that night.

- **Remind clients that you are never too busy to help the people they care about.** Reiterate that if they have friends, family, or coworkers who are nervous about the market volatility, you are here to help. Encourage them to forward your market update email to their network.

- **Bring up outside accounts.** Make a point to mention to clients that while the accounts you manage are prepared for this correction, now is a good time to review old 401(k)s and other assets you do not currently manage to assess risk.

Choose Your Weapon: Types of Content

Advisors getting started with a content marketing strategy often get hung up on which type of content they should be creating. You can try each of the following types of content to see which resonates best with your network:

- Blog posts
- Videos
- Charts or graphics
- Podcasts
- Newsletters
- Whitepapers
- eBooks
- Books
- Webinars

However, finding the best content type for you is all about one question: what type of content will you actually create consistently? Commit to creating the same type of content each month and stick to it, no matter what.

CHAPTER 3

Harnessing Technology to Supercharge Your Productivity

IN THE INFORMATION age, the technologies we use daily are the fuel to grow our businesses. A Federal Reserve Paper found that technology use can drive business growth by 3–5 percent per year. Technology can be overwhelming to evaluate, but it has the power to make your days either easy and efficient or difficult and maddening. This chapter covers nine steps that will help you evaluate how you can grow your business using technology.

I always ask which of the following technologies advisors are using:

- **Customer relationship management (CRM)** system for managing clients and prospects – your command center for staying organized and keeping client information at your fingertips.

- **Website and marketing tools** to manage your website, blog, email newsletter, social media, and other marketing communications.

- **Financial planning software** for preparing client reports, creating financial plans, and collaborating with clients on their accounts.

- **Financial research tools** to access data on funds, companies, and markets.

If I ask ten different advisors which of these technologies they use, I'll get five to seven different answers. I know from my experience working with my dad's firm that mistakes in choosing technologies can waste hours of productivity each week and produce incredible headwinds to growth. At worst, they could disrupt your client experience and cause confusion for your clients.

But choosing new technologies for your firm doesn't have to be risky. Take your time in selecting new tools so that you can be confident in your decision, can fully invest in learning how to use them, and have to change systems less frequently.

Have a Clear Process for Selecting Technologies

1. Ask Advisors with Similar Business Models

Some advisors ask which systems the top-producing advisors are using, but these systems may or may not apply to the size and complexity of their own firm. Top advisors may use technologies that are more complex and expensive than an advisor with fewer clients needs. Seek out a few firms that you admire who are the same size or slightly larger than your firm. Chances are, technologies those firms recommend will be a smart fit for you.

2. Consult Your Home Office

Your home office folks will be aware of negotiated price discounts and integrations that may make your life easier. But be wary if they suggest in-house technology providers, as broker-dealers have built some of the most poorly constructed technologies out there.

3. Use a LinkedIn Group to Get Recommendations

I love to pose technology questions within groups because members are quick to share their experience, and you can get a consensus quickly. Most broker-dealers have LinkedIn groups for their advisors where you can browse discussions and ask questions.

4. Make a Shortlist, Then Do a Demo

Get together a list of three to five highly recommended providers for the system you are looking for, then do a one-on-one demo if possible to ask questions and see the tools in action. Take notes of anything you think is lacking or a deal breaker. Compare your notes on your shortlist and you should have a clear winner.

5. Call Customer Service Before You Purchase

I see advisors leave technology providers most often because of service-related problems. Call the customer service department before you purchase to check the wait time as well as their friendliness and capability. Ask a few questions to kick the tires.

6. Check Out the Available Ongoing Education

Check that the technical support and resources fit your needs. If you are the type of person who prefers to watch how-to videos, make sure the technology provider you select offers a video library. If you need to pick up the phone and speak with a person, be sure that option is available.

7. Think of the Future

We all plan to grow our businesses in the future. But if you're serious about growing in the double digits each year, make sure your technology can scale with your firm. Evaluate pricing for the configuration that will serve your needs now and at double the size to be sure the price increase won't be prohibitive in the future.

8. Manage Your Risk

All technologies will fail from time to time. If your tablet breaks down before a lunch meeting, your business will survive. But if your clients can't access their accounts for a week, it's a catastrophe. Think through the risk involved if the technology fails and formulate an emergency backup plan if necessary.

9. Take Advantage of the Free Trial

I'm always amazed that it's commonplace to purchase a home to live in for years without having spent a night inside. Taking a test drive is the surest way to find out whether you love or hate a particular technology. Take advantage of any free trial to see how you feel using the tool. If you are excited to use the technology, the features are impressive, and it seems fun to use then you have a winner. If it's overwhelming, complex, or frustrating, you may want to keep evaluating.

10. Immerse Yourself in Learning the New Technology Upfront

Learning a technology well from the start is a lot like investing for retirement early, in that you will continue to reap rewards over the long term. Putting time and energy into learning the basics will make you more proficient and efficient each day you use the new system. You will take advantage of more features, waste less time, and enjoy the process more.

Investing in the Right Technology

If your time is worth $200 per hour, you should be willing to invest up to $200 per month to save just 15 minutes per week. Underinvesting in technology can lead to a frustrating, unproductive business model. Embracing integrated technologies allows you to get more work done from your home or office and on the road.

Be choosy and demanding about the technologies you use in your firm, and don't be afraid to make changes when better alternatives come along. If you get stuck, hire a technology consultant to help you implement and master the best technologies for advisors to stay ahead of the curve.

Step 1: Secure Password Storage

Do you waste valuable time every day searching for passwords or login info? If you're not already using secure password storage software, I implore you to adopt a program such as LastPass to automatically store your passwords today.

LastPass is a password manager that attaches to your web browser, so after you log into your LastPass account, your passwords for each site you visit are automatically entered. You can also store credit card and banking info, generate secure passwords for new accounts, and save them automatically. LastPass will save you minutes each day and hours each month, not to mention plenty of hassle and frustration. The premium version is just $1 per month, so you can't afford not to adopt this time-saver today.

Step 2: A Good Customer Relationship Management System

Every morning, bright and early, I lace up my running shoes to make the 2-mile jog to feed my two beautiful and hungry horses. During my run, I often think about how my advisor clients are growing their businesses. Some unlikely advisors' businesses are booming, and some of my most talented and brilliant clients have trouble moving the needle.

Yesterday, I realized a pattern I had never recognized before. Several of my most tech-savvy advisors are not using a CRM (customer relationship management) system, but almost all of my most technology-challenged advisors use one religiously to store all of the information they need about clients and prospects.

It turns out that disorganized advisors need a CRM to function. As a marketer for my clients, CRMs make my life much easier because my clients who use them are constantly adding new contacts to their system, which grows their email list. They're able to update outdated email addresses easily, so we get more people to open and forward our marketing emails. I have noticed that they also follow up with new leads more reliably and close more business as a result.

CRMs for financial advisors have come a long way in the past 5 years, so if you aren't using one now, it may be time for another look. My clients who do use CRMs tend to feel more confident in the growth of their business, less stressed, and more organized. Because today's CRMs are so easy to use, even advisors who have trouble logging into Facebook can operate their CRM like a pro.

Which CRMs Do Financial Advisors Use?

The most popular CRMs for advisors include Redtail, Salesforce, Wealthbox, and Envestnet. However, many of these CRMs are notoriously clunky and difficult to use. My favorite CRM for advisors is Wealthbox, which was created and designed specifically for our industry and with the average advisor's technology proficiency in mind. Serial wealth management entrepreneur Steven Lockshin and top advisor Michael Kitces worked together to help develop Wealthbox. The company's tagline is "A CRM you'll actually enjoy using," which I find to be true for my clients.

Wealthbox is by far the easiest CRM to use, even for my most technology-challenged advisors. You don't need to complete any trainings to use it because the system is so intuitive. There are no lengthy sales calls or orientations; just sign up and get started. The cost is low, there are no contracts or setup fees, and you can cancel anytime. They even have integrations so you can move your contacts over from Redtail or Salesforce with a few clicks.

Wealthbox is approved by many major broker-dealers and uses bank-level encryption to keep your files, data, and client information safe. It also has team functionality, which means you can give your staff the access they need so you're all on the same page. At just $35 per user per month, it's a no-brainer for advisors who aren't currently using a CRM. If you've ever felt disorganized, like leads are falling through the cracks, or had difficulty finding information about your clients, do yourself a favor and get a CRM today. Here are some of the benefits you'll enjoy.

Organize Your Contacts

Wealthbox allows you to organize all of the information you need about your clients, prospects, and referral partners: their email address, phone number, job title, marital status, family members, etc. You can tag contacts to create email groups. For example, you could add a tag for "local client" and then easily search for all local clients to invite them to an upcoming event.

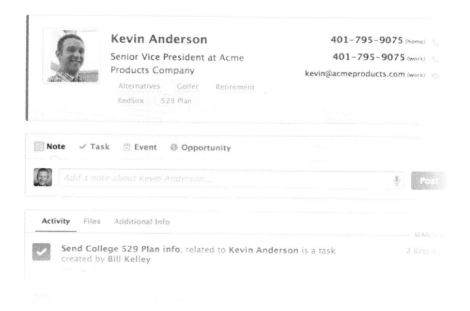

If this is your first CRM, you may need to invest some time in moving your contacts into the system, but if you need guidance, get help from my virtual assistant, who is familiar with the platform (see Step 9).

A CRM will save you time and stress because you're able to pull up information about a contact by searching for their name, employer, family members, job title, etc. All relevant information is available in one place and searchable by keyword, so if you can't remember who works at Qualcomm, you can search for that employer and pull up a list.

Store Important Emails

I know too many advisors today that waste time searching for the information they need in their old emails. With email dropbox, you can securely store your important email correspondence with clients for future reference, and emails are automatically connected to your client's CRM record.

Save Background Information and Notes

Most CRMs are designed to help salespeople make more sales, which often requires having more than just barebones information about their leads. You can add background info, notes, and other reminders that you'll find helpful to review before your calls or meetings. After each phone call, type up a few notes you can revisit before you next speak to your client to jog your memory.

Set Appointments and Reminders

Wealthbox integrates with your existing calendar, so you can easily remind yourself of things you need to accomplish or upcoming meetings. You can add reminders for tasks you need to complete for each client and assign them a priority level and due date. The Wealthbox calendar shows your past and future annual review appointments and notes all in one place.

Save Files to the Cloud

Another benefit is the ability to securely save files to the cloud. You can search for documents by keyword, maintain a secure file backup, and keep annual reports linked to each client's profile. This is helpful if you don't have a rock-solid file system in place or if you'd like to remove sensitive files from your computer and keep backups.

Keep Track of Leads

A CRM allows you to track leads so you can follow up with them and improve your closing rate. You can add each new opportunity to Wealthbox and even include their account size, probability of closing, expected close date, and next step reminders. This can help you forecast future revenue and remind you to follow up so no opportunities slip through the cracks.

Access Everything on Your Mobile Device

One big advantage of using Wealthbox is that have secure access to all of your files, contacts, phone numbers, email addresses, notes, and calendars from your mobile device. The mobile app is easy to use and keeps all of your information in one place when you're on the go.

Integrate with Other Systems

Wealthbox integrates with major technologies for advisors such as eMoney, MoneyGuidePro, Riskalyze, and Orion.

Step 3: Financial Planning Software

Offering financial planning software is key for client retention and can save you time because clients can better access and manage their own accounts. These tools help you focus on comprehensive financial planning, by giving clients access to:

- Budgeting tools
- Spending analysis
- Goal-based savings plans
- Secure document storage
- Scenario-planning and decision-making tools

Tools such as eMoney and MoneyGuidePro offer client login to view investment performance, reports, estate planning tools, "what if" planning, and more.

Step 4: A Robo Platform

When a client or prospect with an account lower than your minimum approaches you, what do you do? A robo platform such as Betterment for Advisors offers a seamless, automated solution for opening, onboarding, and managing these accounts. It guides your clients through a personalized account setup, features automatic trading, rebalancing, and tax-loss harvesting, and lets clients set up their own automatic deposits and withdrawals.

Step 5: An Online Appointment Scheduler

Online appointment scheduling software allows someone to click a link and view available spots on your calendar in order to book a time that works for them. The software syncs with your email, CRM, or other online calendar to show when you're busy and when you're free. When someone books a meeting, the appointment is automatically added to your calendar and the time is marked as busy.

Rarely do I come across a technology that can both save us time and make us money. If you've ever set up a phone call with me, you know I'm fond of my virtual meeting scheduler. It saves me from going back and forth by email to find a time that works for everyone. It also allows prospects to get on my calendar quickly or during non-business hours, before their sense of urgency wanes.

An online appointment scheduler helps the advisors I work with streamline their scheduling process, convert more leads, and get more done during meetings. If you haven't set up an online calendar, take 15 minutes to change your life today!

There are three popular software providers: ScheduleOnce, TimeTrade, and Calendly. All three are good options, but I recommend Calendly for one very important reason: I think it's the most fun to use. The free version of Calendly provides unlimited meetings and syncs with Outlook, Office, and Google Calendar.

The big three offer similar features, including:

- Setting busy or available hours
- Offering various meeting lengths
- Adding a time buffer between appointments
- Allowing you to confirm a meeting before it's scheduled
- Advance alerts for new meetings

My dad still uses a paper appointment book, so to set up his online calendar, we blocked off a few hours each week for him to be available for meetings set up online. We chose Tuesday and Thursday from 3:30 to 6:30 p.m., when he's normally at the driving range. He marks his paper calendar as busy during this time and gets an email notice 24 hours in advance if someone books a call online.

Benefits of Online Scheduling

1. Save Time

The most obvious and immediate benefit of online appointment scheduling is that you will save hours of going back and forth by email or playing phone tag to find a suitable time for a meeting. Instead, you can share a link to your calendar and allow contacts to schedule a time that works for them. They can easily add the meeting to their calendar once it's booked.

Philip Board, a top client of mine in Upland, California, explains, "When we're speaking to a client trying to book a meeting they often say, 'My spouse isn't home right now, can I get back to you?' We send them the link so they can cross-reference their calendars and bam! The meeting shows up on our calendar."

2. Generate More Leads

Scheduling a phone call online is an easy, low-stakes way for prospects to take the next step with you. If they're reading a blog post or visiting your website after hours, they're much more likely to schedule a phone call online than they are to remember to call you the next day. Once you have your scheduler set up, add it as a call to action for each blog post or marketing email you send out.

Advisor Philip Board has had success with new prospects scheduling a phone call on his website: "The link on the website has been used with new prospects for initial consultations. I'm surprised wholesalers haven't figured out it's an easy way to get to my calendar, but until they do it's an invaluable tool for prospects."

3. Get More Done During Meetings

When clients schedule a call in advance, you can better prepare for the meeting. You are able to review the latest updates to their accounts and have their information at the ready, as opposed to when the phone rings and catches you off guard.

4. Have Fewer In-Person Meetings

Advisors who have adopted online meeting schedulers find that when clients can quickly book a phone call anytime, they opt for fewer in-person meetings. This means less time spent commuting to and participating in face-to-face meetings that could be quickly conducted over the phone.

5. Stay on the Cutting Edge

As we all grow more accustomed to technology and your client base gets younger, having online appointment access will become more important. Philip Board believes the trend will continue: "I think as we move into the next generation of clients, they will expect to have something like this available to them. Many of our clients still love to hear from us by phone and mail, but having the option online makes things easy for them."

How to Set Up and Use Your Scheduler

Go to Calendly.com, create an account by typing in your email address, and click the link to "Get Started for Free." Once you've set up your scheduler and synced it with your existing calendar, you'll want to make it easy for people to use. I recommend adding a link to your website, marketing materials, blog posts, and email signature. Be sure to keep the link handy so you can send it within an email to folks requesting a meeting time. When encouraging people to book online, I usually write, "Please use this link to schedule a call or suggest some times that work for you," so they have a choice of scheduling the old-fashioned way if they prefer.

Step 6: Google Analytics

Google Analytics is the free, industry-standard solution to view statistics about the traffic to your website and valuable data linked to those numbers, such as visitor behavior. Tracking your analytics will answer these questions:

- How much traffic did your website get last month?
- Which pages received the most traffic?
- Which of your blog posts were the most popular?

- How much of your traffic came from social media?
- Where should you spend more marketing dollars?

Step 7: Riskalyze

Riskalyze is the technology I wish I had built. It offers a clear, quantitative way to communicate with clients about risk. It's also a sales tool that can be hosted front and center on your website to convert prospects.

The brazen marketing slogan of the company is "Show prospects they're invested wrong. Prove to clients they're invested right." Riskalyze is a great tool for reviewing the inherent tradeoff between risk and reward.

For example, your client Linda is extremely risk averse and insists on being invested ultra-conservatively. When her long-lost brother Matt takes a look at her portfolio, he tells her that she hasn't earned enough over the past year and she ought to fire her financial advisor. Using her Riskalyze questionnaire, you can gently remind Linda that her risk score is 22 and that to have gotten an 11 percent return last year, she would have needed to invest like an 84. The tool provides a framework for managing expectations and understanding your clients' risk profiles.

One recent bonus of Riskalyze is their new "Auto-Pilot" robo offering, where clients can automatically transfer small accounts to be managed by a third party with very low fees in a portfolio that matches their risk tolerance. Auto-pilot can neutralize the robo threat for you. It is a great solution for children of clients just starting out or smaller referral accounts you normally couldn't take on.

Step 8: Share Your Screen (For Free!)

Do you find yourself wishing you could share your computer screen or see your client's computer screen during phone calls? When clients are having trouble accessing their accounts online or have a question about their investments, you can use screen sharing technology to get on the same (web) page.

I use Join.me all the time to explain my marketing services to prospects and support my sales calls. I also use screen sharing to host small group trainings and webinars. Join.me provides conference calling capabilities with each meeting, so participants can dial in to hear the audio of the meeting (if you don't have your own dedicated conference line). Meeting participants can type to chat and ask questions. You can hand over the "presenter" role to another meeting participant to share their screen. And they can give you control of their cursor so you can solve technical issues on their computer.

A free Join.me account allows up to ten meeting participants at once, but recording calls, handing over the presenter role, and controlling the cursor are paid features.

One advantage of Join.me, compared with alternative screen sharing tools, is that anyone can access your meeting using their Internet browser without logging in or downloading any software. This is helpful when clients are feeling stuck or are having technical issues. And don't worry, your meetings are "locked," and you approve each participant before they can join the meeting and see your screen.

What the client will see:

What you will see:

Most often, the advisors I work with use Join.me when a client calls with a question or a technology issue. While on the phone with the client, the advisor directs them to their custom link (ours is join.me/IndigoMarketingAgency) to enter the meeting. You can use the online meeting to share audio, but it's often easier to stay on the phone and use the online meeting for screen sharing only. On the shared screen, you can review educational materials with clients, show them investment information and market updates, or explain how to fill out forms.

It only takes a few minutes to get up and running with your own free Join.me account. Once you click to sign up, an automated prompt will take you through the setup steps.

Step 9: Hire a Virtual Assistant

This is one tip that I believe will change your life and your business. It certainly helped me grow my business and significantly reduced my stress level 4 years ago when I hired my first professional virtual assistant. Now I have four assistants for different personal, professional, and business tasks.

While the number of advisors who are working as part of a team has increased by 25 percent in the past 4 years, the majority of independent advisors are still one-man shops, working independently without any support staff. Barron's reports that many advisors make the transition to a team when they approach $100 million in AUM.

How Many Hours per Week Are You Working as a Financial Advisor?

Working on your own has many benefits, but one of the downsides is that you have to do everything yourself, and your productivity suffers as a result. The most valuable use of your time is meeting with clients and creating financial plans, but when you run your own business, the majority of your time is spent elsewhere.

What would you say to one of your top clients, a physician struggling to retire on time, who told you he was only working in his practice 4 days a week because he needed 1 day each week to mow his lawn and maintain his yard? You'd surely urge him to hire a gardener to free up his valuable time to earn 25 percent more! Hiring a virtual assistant offers the same benefit for a financial advisor, putting more hours of your week into tasks with the highest profitability.

Think about the work you did this week. How many hours did you spend working as a financial advisor on tasks that generate maximum revenue? Are you productive or busy?

The most successful advisors I work with are without a doubt the ones who have a support staff. Whether they're part of a larger firm with full-time team members or a one-man shop with a good virtual assistant, top performers know how to get the help they need.

I hired my first virtual assistant after reading the bestseller *The 4-Hour Workweek*. Author Tim Ferriss built his empire on outsourcing repetitive or menial tasks to keep his time focused on writing books and growing his businesses. "Doing less meaningless work so that you can focus on things of greater importance is not laziness," Ferriss says. "We need to focus on being productive, instead of being busy."

In another classic, *Getting Things Done: The Art of Stress-Free Productivity*, David Allen encourages people to delegate everything they can to increase productivity. "You can do anything, but you can't do everything. Sometimes the biggest gain in productivity comes from clearing your desk." By having an avenue to outsource meaningless tasks, you free up your time for the big initiatives. Virtual assistants provide a pressure valve to reduce your workload of urgent but non-critical work.

What Is a Virtual Assistant?

A virtual assistant is a professional who provides administrative or technical support to their clients remotely. Whereas hiring a full-time administrative assistant may cost you $50,000 per year plus benefits, virtual assistants bill hourly as contractors, so you are not responsible for employee-related taxes, insurance, or benefits. What's more, virtual assistants bill you only for the time they actually work, so you don't waste money on idle employees.

Professional virtual assistants are highly trained and experienced problem solvers familiar with time-saving technologies and productivity strategies. I find that my own virtual assistants complete complex tasks in much less time than it would take me – and often with better results. Because they're highly organized and laser-focused on individual tasks, virtual assistants make sure everything is completed on time and nothing falls through the cracks.

How Do Financial Advisors Use Virtual Assistants?

I first saw advisors using virtual assistants years ago as appointment setters. Some advisors started out hiring an answering service to answer their calls while they were away from the office. But today, most advisors I know use virtual assistants to do technology and administrative work.

Here are some examples of tasks my virtual assistant service has helped advisor clients with this week:

- Adding prospects' email addresses to a database
- Making changes to the advisor's website
- Calling prospects to remind them of an upcoming event
- Troubleshooting technology issues
- Making required compliance changes to documents
- Updating social media profiles
- Proofreading and editing communications
- Making dinner reservations and finding nearby parking
- Researching flights and hotels for an upcoming conference

The beauty of working with a talented virtual assistant is that you can easily get things off your plate as soon as they come into your mind. Those nagging to-do lists and problems you meant to solve can be crossed off with a short email. And don't be afraid to outsource personal tasks; it makes no difference to the virtual assistant and can often save you hours and reduce stress.

What to Look For in a Virtual Assistant

We're all wary of the $4 per hour virtual assistants working from the Philippines. I recommend finding a professional virtual assistant in your area so you can meet them in person and review references before hiring. My top virtual assistant, Tammy, lives near me in San Diego and is a personal friend. She has worked as an executive assistant, productivity coach, and professional virtual assistant for years. We meet every few months in person to review our projects and brainstorm how we can work together more efficiently.

To find a qualified professional, try a LinkedIn search for "virtual assistant" in your area. Interview at least three candidates and speak with their references. Be sure the assistant is proficient in the technologies that you use. My virtual assistants are trained to use the following platforms:

- FMG Suite
- WordPress
- Advisor Websites
- Erado and Smarsh
- Redtail
- Salesforce
- LinkedIn, Facebook, and Twitter
- Riskalyze

How Much Does a Virtual Assistant Cost?

Of course, you get what you pay for with any professional you hire. Instead of focusing on the hourly rate, I recommend focusing on technical proficiencies and stellar references. The goal of hiring a virtual assistant is to save you time, so you want to work with someone who is experienced with the technologies you're using and won't require you to answer a lot of questions for them to complete each task.

I have worked with several types of virtual assistants, with positive results. My most important or complex tasks go to my top assistant, who charges $50 per hour. She is a tenacious problem solver who doesn't give up when troubleshooting issues to find intelligent long-term solutions. My less complex and more repetitive tasks go to another assistant with razor-sharp attention to detail and follow-through, who charges $25 per hour. The very time-consuming tasks, such as manually harvesting information from databases or sending LinkedIn messages, go to another assistant, who charges $12 per hour.

If you're a financial advisor just getting started using a virtual assistant, you can expect to pay $30–40 per hour, and I recommend hiring the best help you can afford. Confidently outsourcing work that gets done correctly the first time is worth the investment. Because virtual assistants are often more productive than you would be at completing the same task, you can expect to free up one afternoon of your time for around $100. What kind of impact could you make on your business with one quiet afternoon per week to focus?

But the true value of a good virtual assistant isn't in the hours that get put back into your week. It's in the feeling of being able to address issues as soon as they come across your desk, to cross everything off your to-do list by the end of each day, and to think clearly about important projects because you're on top of your urgent obligations.

CHAPTER 4
Get a Website with Horsepower

I BROUGHT ON two new clients this month with websites so bad I felt a flash of red-hot embarrassment when I first saw them. Marketing efforts are crippled by a bad website, so I encouraged them to do a website overhaul. One said they were going to do an update in 2021, and the other said they were going to have their brother-in-law look into building a new site.

This reminded me of an article I had been writing for one of my advisors encouraging his clients to stop putting off their estate planning. He had a set of clients with three children and no estate plan in place. He was alarmed that they had not documented a guardian for their children in the event of their death or designated assets toward that cost. They were stuck hemming and hawing over which child should get which fine china.

Advisors with outdated websites sometimes behave in the same way. They view a website redesign as a soul-searching rebranding process that will dictate the operations of their firm into the future. Don't let perfectionism stop you from making an overdue update to your site. In reality, website updates should happen every 2–3 years, or as often as required to take account of major changes, and should take less than 30 days, start to finish.

By outsourcing to a professional who is familiar with your industry, you can save time and make the process go more smoothly. Please do not employ your kids or another relative to create your site. This is akin to your biggest client calling you to rebalance her account based on an investment tip from her dead-beat brother. Website developers are talented, educated professionals who employ best practices and the latest technologies. They can create a better site much more quickly than someone who dabbles. They are widely available at a low cost, so do yourself and your relatives a favor and outsource to a pro.

Step 1: Create a Secure and Responsive Website

There are several options when it comes to building your new site. You'll want to consider your compliance situation, budget, and technical expertise when deciding which platform to use. We now provide website services at Indigo Marketing, so you can take a look at what we offer! We've worked with some of the leading website platforms for financial advisors for years. With increasing prices, reduced service, and outdated technologies, we decided it was time to create a better solution at a lower price. How? By leveraging the most powerful independent website technology in the world: WordPress.

I have worked with hundreds of financial advisors using every major website provider and concluded that FMG Suite is also great for functionality, site designs, pricing, and ease of use. If you are affiliated with one of the larger broker-dealers that has a compliance integration with FMG Suite, then using their platform is a no-brainer because it makes compliance so easy. If you regularly blog or host events, they have features for both that are simple to use.

There are other advantages to using a large website company such as FMG Suite, Advisor Websites, or Advisor Launchpad (formerly Smarsh Sites). They routinely make updates to their platform, so your site will be upgraded as technology changes. Their sites are mobile responsive and meet the latest technical requirements. By choosing a financial services–specific provider, you won't have to worry about issues such as adding the required BrokerCheck link to your site. Finally, a few years down the line, when you're ready for a facelift, you can choose one of their newer themes and update your site seamlessly.

SSL Certificates

Things change quickly in the world of websites and digital marketing. Something you may have been hearing a lot about lately is SSL certificates. But what is an SSL certificate? And does your site really need one? Go to your site and look in the upper-left corner of the browser address bar; if there's a warning that your site is not secure, then you don't have an SSL certificate. This is unfortunate because it erodes trust with your website visitors and keeps your site from getting as much traffic as possible.

Secure socket layer (SSL) certificates are small data files that create a secure connection between your website and a visitor's computer. This prevents hackers or malware from intercepting any information entered on your website. Securing your site also changes your website prefix from HTTP: to HTTPS: and displays a "Secure" padlock icon next to your website's address.

Hackers are creative and innovative. If your website is not secure, they have inventive ways to try to trick your visitors, such as displaying an image encouraging them to click on a link to enter sensitive financial information that will be intercepted by the hacker.

Only the owner of a website and its domain can purchase an SSL certificate for the site. In this way, securing your site tells search engines that you are who you say you are and that your site is representing a legitimate business. This is why search engines give more credibility to sites with certificates installed.

Years ago, SSL certificates were required only for websites where users entered sensitive information or made online purchases. But today, Google and other search engines are cracking down on cybersecurity and putting more emphasis on websites installing SSL certificates.

In summary, installing an SSL certificate:

- Removes the "not secure" warning from your website
- Creates a secure connection to protect your site visitors from hackers
- Gaining trust and credibility with website visitors
- Improves your search engine optimization and gets more traffic to your site

The good news is that it's relatively easy and inexpensive to get an SSL certificate for your website. GoDaddy sells them for $69 per year. You can purchase your certificate and ask your web developer to install it for you. Be sure to check with your website provider first to make sure they can support an SSL certificate.

Step 2: Add Custom Content to Attract a Relevant Audience

I come across a lot of advisors who maintain separate websites and blogs. This is not advisable from a search engine optimization (SEO) or marketing perspective. SEO is impacted by traffic to your site and by new content on your site, so adding your blog to your main website will help with SEO for both. Also, you will want clients and prospects who visit your website to peruse your blog, so featuring it on your website's navigation bar helps drive more traffic to your posts.

Most financial advisors really need help writing their websites, but there are only a handful of firms that offer website copywriting for financial advisors. That's because it's difficult to create a personal and powerful message that's also SEO and compliance friendly.

Here are our key tips on how to write a great website.

Your Homepage Can Make or Break Your Marketing

When was the last time you updated the copy on your homepage? This task may not be on the top of your to-do list, but everyone needs strong copy on their website to explain what they do, who they serve, and how they help. Most advisors make a critical mistake with this piece of prime real estate: *They talk about themselves!*

Can you imagine if you went into a retail store and the sales associate started off by telling you about himself? You would lose interest right away. Yet most advisors use the most important area of their website to list boring things about their firm.

One powerful but simple change you can make to your site is to update your headline to focus on your potential clients. *What is the one urgent problem that you solve for a specific group?* (Remember, you answered this question in Chapter 1.) Feature the benefits people get from working with you front and center on your site. This generates a much more memorable and powerful emotional response from your website visitors.

Let's take a look at what most advisors' websites say. I can't tell you how many sites I see every day that list *comprehensive financial planning, fiduciary, or fee-only* as the advisor's big differentiator. What's meant to set you apart is actually making you look exactly like every other advisor in your town.

If I Google "Financial Advisor San Diego" and take the top three search results, here's what I find (I'm not kidding):

- "Experience the Pure Difference: Fee-only financial planning to set you on track for the journey that lies ahead"

- "Dorn Financial. We are fee-only financial planners located in San Diego, California"

- "Blue Water Capital Management, LLC: Financial Planning and Investment Management. Independent. Fee-Only. Fiduciary"

If you were looking for a financial advisor, which of these firms would you want to work with? It would be impossible to choose, because all three sound exactly the same. We know nothing about what makes them different, who they serve, or how they help.

Contrast that experience with a formula to help your website stand out from the crowd: Change your homepage headline to explain the main benefit you offer to the specific group you serve. Here are a few real-life examples from advisors:

- "Helping Business Owners Exit Their Firms and Retire with True Wealth"

- "Helping Qualcomm Employees Maximize Their Retirement & Benefits Package"

- "Creating a Plan for Your Divorce Settlement to Provide Income for Life"

Featuring the core benefit you offer to your clients on your homepage captures interest, creates an emotional connect, and helps you stand out from the crowd. Give it a try. Update your site today then keep track of how it performs over the next 30 days.

Create Trust in the "About" Section

After the homepage, a financial advisor's "About" page typically gets the most views. Clients and prospects want to know who the advisor is and what makes them tick. An advisor's "About" page should feature a healthy balance of personal story and details about their expertise and experience, balancing the heart and the head.

When writing your story, share more than your business experience and credentials. Dive into your passion for the industry and what you enjoy most about your job. If you were inspired to become a financial advisor by a specific person or incident, share your motivation.

This page is often either the easiest or the most difficult page for advisors to write. For some, sharing their story is simple and exciting and the words will flow onto the page. For others, determining how to tell their story or what to include can cause uncertainty. You may be asking yourself, "Am I oversharing? How much is too much? Will anyone really care?"

Because this page is so personal and it's tough to write about yourself, it often helps to have a professional writer tell your story. Take a look at one advisor's original "About" page and the page that we recently created:

Before:

First, as a registered representative of LPL Financial, and now, as an Investment Advisor Representative of LPL Financial, I provide professional investment advisory services to more than 150 individual clients who have more than $65,000,000 invested with me in securities through LPL Financial.

After:

Thanks for visiting my website and learning more about why I became a financial advisor. I have lived in San Diego all of my life, growing up in a small house in Lemon Grove, with two brothers and working-class parents. My father served in the Navy for 40 years and my mother worked as a caterer and a baker while she raised me and my two younger brothers. Like many in the 1940s and 1950s, we experienced some difficult times and struggled to make ends meet.

I realized from a young age the sense of peace, security, and dignity that successful financial planning can provide. This inspired me to eventually enter the financial services industry and help people just like my parents feel confident in their financial situation and give security to their families.

Early in my career, I saw firsthand how I could help people by guiding them toward security and confidence in their future. I committed my career to working with positive individuals who want to plan and invest for the long-term and, over the past 36 years, this goal has transformed into my life's passion.

Today, I remain committed to educating, engaging, and inspiring as many people as possible to take control of their finances. I enjoy building close, long-lasting relationships with my clients, many of which span decades and generations.

Over the years I have noticed that clients frequently call me to share their happy news, whether it's a new job or the birth of a child. I am also honored to serve as a shoulder to lean on during difficult times in life, such as a layoff, divorce, or death. It's my privilege to help clients on their personal journeys and to celebrate their successes with them. I look forward to meeting you to learn more about your goals and dreams.

Clients and prospects can't trust you until they understand why you do what you do. Sharing your personal story can help people relate to you and feel more comfortable sharing their story with you.

Embrace Your Specialty throughout Your Copy

It's important to share your specialties through the copy on your website so that visitors feel like you will understand their unique challenges. If you work with three specific niches, include all three on your homepage. This could, for example, mean mentioning professionals in the science and medical fields, women, and small business owners. Don't be shy about explaining exactly who you serve best.

If you're worried about alienating potential clients that do not fit into your specialty, be sure to list both a broad and a narrow focus, such as "Helping families plan for retirement and Chevron employees maximize their benefits." Embracing a specialization may be counterintuitive, but it's the only way to stand out from the crowd.

Customize Your Photography to Create Trust

Most of the advisors I work with are true specialists, so they want their website and brand, presentations, and social media profiles to be truly unique. The best way to make an impact through your marketing imagery is with original photography of you, your office, and your team.

One advisor here in San Diego, Tim Dyer of Dyer Wealth Management, does an incredible job of featuring original photography throughout his website.

Tim hired an excellent local photographer to shoot a variety of photos to feature throughout his marketing. For example, when Tim writes a blog post about his unique process for working with clients, instead of using a stock photo, he uses a photo of himself actually meeting with clients.

Similarly, instead of using a generic photo on the team page of his website, he features a high-quality image of his team meeting in the conference room as the banner image. Most of the images on his website are photos of his office and team. This adds a personal touch to the site and lets prospects "meet" him and his team.

Where to Use Your Photography

Investing in high-quality original photography can take time, effort, and money. To maximize the return on this investment, you can plan to use your photography consistently across all branded collateral including:

- Your website
- Social media profiles
- Blog posts
- Google Business Profile
- Brochures
- PowerPoint presentations
- Reports
- Print and digital advertisements

Tips for Getting Amazing Photographs

If you invest in original photography, make sure your session is a success. Here are some tips for shooting a great collection of photographs you can use in your marketing for years to come:

1. Think beyond the Headshot

Of course you need a great headshot for your website and social media pro-files, but by featuring artful imagery of your office and team throughout your website and marketing collaterals, you can add depth and interest. Be sure you have images in both landscape and portrait orientation with lots of extra space around the subjects and taken from a variety of angles.

Here are a few types of photos to capture:

- Conservative headshot
- Casual headshot
- Candid profile
- Meeting with clients
- Office images
- Team photos
- Website background images

2. Get Creative

Don't be afraid to get creative and try out different ideas. If you don't like how the image looks, you don't have to use it. Try a mixture of candid and posed shots in several locations around the office, such as the conference room, the lobby, and your personal office. You can also have the photographer take a few shots of your office without any people present.

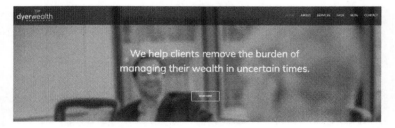

3. Invest in a Talented Photographer

The first step to getting great photos is to hire a talented, experienced photographer. Ask around or use Yelp.com to find some great business photographers. Then get quotes and request samples of their work. Choose the highest-quality photographer you can afford, since the bigger investment will be your time and energy.

A novice photographer wouldn't have been able to capture this beautiful reflection of Tim's logo in his conference room:

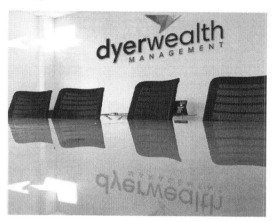

Need help locating a top-notch photographer in your area? Email our virtual assistant Tammy at tammy@indigomarketingagency.com and she'll find you three great candidates for $100 or less.

4. Go Outside

Once you have photos of your team and your office, get some outdoor photos. Everyone looks better outdoors, and greenery adds interest to photography. Try your office courtyard or a public park or garden.

5. Don't Be Afraid to Travel

Many of our offices aren't the most photogenic settings, but don't fret if you don't have a gorgeous building nearby. Take a field trip to a hotel or museum to get interesting and striking images that make you look great. Hotel lobbies often have beautiful but understated artwork and decor that can provide the perfect backdrop for your shoot.

Using Your Photos

Once the photographer sends you the final images, choose between twelve and twenty photos that you love. Add them to your website pages and social media, and start integrating them into your other marketing materials for cohesive branding. There's no need to update the photos for at least 10 years, with the exception of your headshot, which should be updated every 5 years.

Step 3: Add Conversion Tools

Have you snooped around top advisors' websites recently to see what they have in common? In addition to excellent branding and site design, top-performing websites include several key features that help them attract and convert more qualified prospects. In my work with hundreds of top advisors, I've identified five key features of top-performing advisor websites. Does your website have all five?

1. A Sample Financial Plan

Most advisors forget that at the end of the day, the product they're selling is financial planning. It makes sense that potential clients are interested in seeing what they're considering purchasing from your firm. Yet very few advisors feature a sample financial plan on their website.

Create a page explaining your process and what's included, with a PDF of your sample plan available for download. Then take it a step further and add a button to your homepage directing folks to see a sample plan. Your sample plan will become one of the most visited pages on your site.

2. A Lead Capture Form

You may not know it, but your site likely gets visits from tens or even hundreds of prospects each month. The problem is that most of these leads go cold before they ever make contact with you. To convert more of them into clients, it's critical to have a lead capture form on your website. A lead capture form is a tool that encourages prospects to enter their email address to sign up for your newsletter, download a report, or watch a video.

To make your lead capture form even stronger, offer a highly valuable report to your prospects. If you work with employees of a specific employer, a report on how to maximize their benefits is relevant and effective. If you work with people in a certain industry, an industry report will work wonders.

3. A Calendar Appointment Scheduler

If a referral is browsing your website at 8 p.m., do you make it easy for them to take the next step while they're feeling a sense of urgency? Most advisors don't. Adding a calendar scheduler to your site allows prospects to take the next step immediately, at any time of the day or night. An added bonus is that a calendar scheduler will save you time scheduling phone calls and appointments with existing clients.

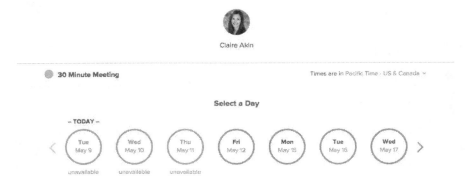

Once you have your online calendar scheduler set up, link to it at the end of each blog post to encourage prospects to make an appointment. (My favorite scheduler is Calendly.) You can add a pop-up scheduler to your website: take a look at the bottom right corner of my website to see how this works. Some top advisors feature several "Schedule an Appointment" buttons on their homepage to get prospects to make an appointment while their interest is piqued.

4. A Custom Video

Research shows that when people are evaluating a financial advisor, they are trying to decide whether they like and trust the advisor. A custom video of you on your site is critical to helping them understand your story and get to know you. Top advisors feature a video of themselves prominently on their website's homepage. Be sure the video features you speaking to the camera. Tell your story and what motivates you to connect with potential clients.

5. A Compelling Call to Action

One of the most important marketing strategies I help advisors create is a compelling call to action (CTA). When your target demographic is presented with your call to action, do they act? If not, your marketing is rotten at its core. So many advisors have amazing websites and content marketing, but they are wasting their opportunities without a call to action that converts.

The best marketing in the world cannot be effective if your call to action is ho-hum. Yet most advisors don't have an offer that *inspires action*. The most common call to action for advisors is "Call now," "Learn more," or "Sign up for our newsletter." If you are using one of these on your website, you know how unsuccessful it is.

If you do one thing for your marketing this year, create a call to action that inspires people to take the next step. It's easy to tell when you have a call to action that's working because prospects will take you up on your offer. The trick is finding a unique, valuable, and motivating offer for your target clients.

What Is a Call to Action?

"Call to action" is marketing lingo for an offer that is designed to motivate action or make a sale. Traditional calls to action are offers like:

- Call now
- Buy now
- Visit our store

For financial advisors, this usually translates into something like:

- Get your portfolio risk analysis
- Get your free financial review

- Learn more now
- Sign up for our newsletter

The problem with these calls to action is that they're not specific to the audience, they don't offer compelling value, and they put the burden on the buyer to do the work.

So often I see advisors with calls to action that focus on their mission statement, their process, or their firm. Website visitors will act only if you are solving an *urgent and painful problem* for them. Focus on their most pressing concerns and offer an easy way for them to take the next step and sleep better tonight.

A good call to action offers valuable benefits to the specific buyer and is incredibly easy to complete. For example, one CTA on my website is "Click to schedule a free 15-minute phone call to get specific marketing recommendations for your advisory firm." It takes less than 10 seconds for someone to complete, and it offers valuable benefits tailored to their business.

Examples of Great CTAs

The best CTAs are specific to a particular group, solve an urgent problem, and take less than 1 minute to complete. Here are three of my favorites from great advisors:

1. Can You Sell Your Business and Buy Financial Freedom?

    One advisor, who serves business owners thinking about selling their companies, offers a short survey titled "How Much Will Financial Freedom Cost You?"

    In just six questions, potential clients find out what their annual cashflow needs will be in retirement, what lump sum they'd need to support that cashflow, and whether they might be able to sell their existing business to buy that financial freedom.

    For an overworked and burnt-out business owner, the answer to that question is pretty compelling. What if financial freedom is closer than they think? Once business owners have self-qualified themselves as being able to sell their firm for enough to retire with the lifestyle they desire, they can work with the advisor to learn how he can help them sell their firm.

2. What Is the Cost of Your ADP Retirement Plan?

Two advisors in Georgia focus on helping ADP employees better invest their retirement accounts. The handful of investments within the retirement plan have high fees and low performance. The advisors have developed a quick survey where ADP employees can enter their holdings and find out how much they are paying in fees and how much they can save by getting access to better investments.

The same firm offers a free report on "How to Maximize Your ADP Benefits Package." The report details the retirement savings plan, stock purchase plan, and health savings plan. Highly compensated executives will naturally find this report incredibly valuable and may schedule a phone call to review their specific questions.

3. How a CRNA S Corporation Can Reduce Your FICA Self-Employment Taxes

CRNA Financial Planning is one of my favorite firms because they're laser-focused on who they serve and how they help. Their only clientele is certified registered nurse anesthetists (CRNAs), and if that's not specific enough, they mainly work with CRNAs who own their own anesthesiology practice.

One of their top-performing blog posts is "How a CRNA S Corporation Can Reduce Your FICA Self-Employment Taxes," which was shared 29 times and viewed by 9,219 people on Facebook this month. The offer at the end is for a free 15-minute phone call to get specific recommendations for lowering taxes. Who wouldn't want that? It's a great example of a CTA that is specific, valuable, and easy to complete.

Here are a few other examples of successful CTAs for advisors:

- Schedule your Social Security review phone call
- Get your impaired risk life insurance quote now
- Join us for our retirement planning webinar

- Schedule a 15-minute financial goal-setting phone call
- Find out what you need to do when you turn 65
- Get a quote for your business 401(k) plan

Of course, you'll need to customize your call to action for your firm and services. Spend a few minutes thinking about your prospects, their most pressing concerns, and how they typically like to first engage with you (email, phone call, webinar). You may have CTAs for each of your major services.

Remember, the attributes that help your CTA convert are:

- Specificity
- Value
- Ease of completion

Tailor your CTA to a specific group of clients that you help, offer tremendous value for free, and aim for the action to take less than 60 seconds.

Case Study: How One Advisor Upgraded His Website

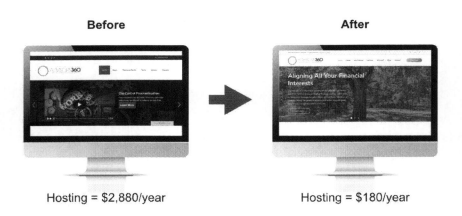

Before   **After**

Hosting = $2,880/year   Hosting = $180/year

We recently completed a website upgrade for a client who had been using an industry-specific hosting platform with a price tag of $240 per month. The advisor decided to move his site because this platform does not provide an SSL certificate and visitors were receiving a warning that read "site is not secure."

He came to us because we build independent websites for financial advisors using WordPress. WordPress is the largest independent website platform in the world: more than 20 percent of the Internet's websites are on WordPress. The platform unlocks tremendous marketing power at an impressively low price. WordPress hosting with an SSL security certificate costs only around $15 per month. For our client, that meant **saving $2,700 in the first year alone!**

Our clients own their WordPress websites outright. They are free to do as they please with them, and no one can turn their site off. Independent sites make sense for independent advisors.

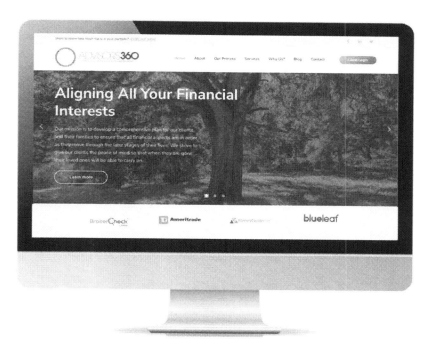

Step 1: Create a Secure and Responsive Website

It's critical that any website in 2019 be both secure and mobile responsive. This allows your website to:

- Perform better in search (SEO)
- Provide a better experience for users (higher conversion)
- Inspire greater trust

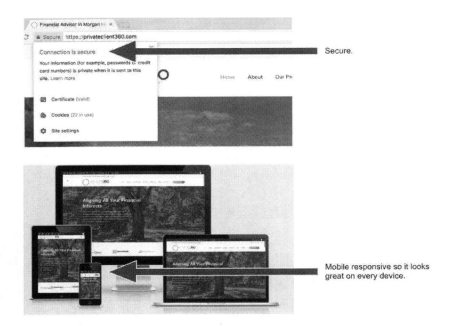

Secure.

Mobile responsive so it looks great on every device.

Step 2: Add Custom Content to Attract a Relevant Audience

After working with thousands of advisors over the past 3 years, we know that advisors with a specialty have a much easier time marketing their business and attracting new clients.

Understand what the firm is about in less than 2 seconds.

Custom photography that matches brand or location.

Authority bars helps establish trust.

Video about the firm.

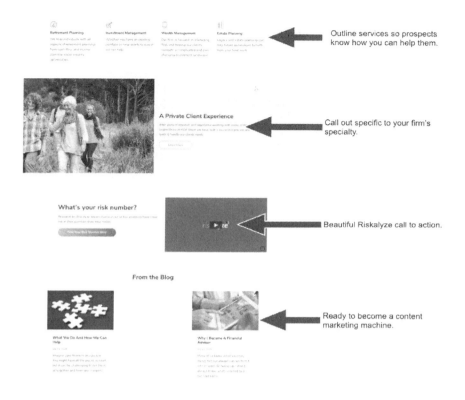

Outline services so prospects know how you can help them.

Call out specific to your firm's specialty.

Beautiful Riskalyze call to action.

Ready to become a content marketing machine.

Step 3: Add Lead Generation Tools

We use a variety of lead generation strategies and install the most popular lead generation tools for advisors on our sites.

Beautiful Riskalyze call to action.

The end result was a better website: secure, mobile responsive, and customized to the advisor's demographic. The cost saving of more than $2,500 per year was the cherry on top!

Whatever solution you choose for your website, make sure you're proud of it. Advisors who are unhappy with their websites tend not to share them as much with clients and prospects, and their marketing suffers as a result. When you have a website that truly captures who you are, what makes you different, and the benefits of working with you, you'll naturally want to share it with everyone you meet.

CHAPTER 5
Install Google Analytics and Upgrade Your Search Engine Optimization (SEO)

PLEASE DON'T SKIP this chapter just because you don't understand the words in the title! You're a financial advisor, which means you understand far more complex topics (Modern Portfolio Theory) than a little bit of geek-speak about how the Internet works. I promise to simplify this chapter so that you're not overwhelmed and no longer embarrassed that you don't understand Google Analytics or SEO.

What Is Google Analytics?

Google Analytics is the most widely used tool in the world to analyze the traffic coming to a website. It's free and it can be connected to any website. It's like a portfolio analysis software for your website.

Most financial advisors have a strong aversion to trying to understand their website's metrics through Google Analytics. Why is this, when we know advisors tend to be numbers driven and analytical in nature? My best guess is that it's because Google Analytics is jargon-rich, confusing, and overwhelming. Because Google Analytics tries to provide users with all the data they'll ever need, it can be difficult to sift through the analytics platform and find meaning in the numbers.

However, you may be more inclined to use Google Analytics when you realize that you really only need to know four things about your website when getting started:

1. How many visitors are coming to your website?

2. Where are your visitors located?

3. What are visitors doing on your site?

4. How did visitors get to your site?

How Many Visitors Are Coming to Your Website?

1. Log into Google Analytics

2. Select the website you want to evaluate and click on "All Website Data"

3. In the top-right dropdown menu, select a date range (try the past 30 days)

4. Go to "Audience," then "Overview" to view "Users"

This answers the question "How many visitors are coming to your site?" For our example advisor, 381 users have visited the site in the past month. That's not terrible, considering this is the advisor's old site that has not been optimized for SEO and has no integrated marketing. However, in the next step we will quickly learn that the total traffic does not tell the whole story.

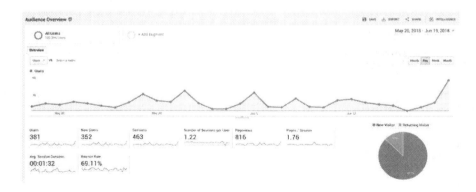

Where Are Your Visitors Located?

This is where it starts to get interesting – or disheartening, if you are our advisor. To answer this question, go to "Audience," then "Geo," then "Location." You can see from the data here that almost half of our site visitors are from outside the United States. A full 100 are from France! The advisor does not offer financial advice in France, so these are not qualified prospects.

When you click on the name of each country, you'll get more detailed data. For example, of the folks visiting the site from the United States, about 70 percent are from California, which is great, since this is where the advisor does business. Unfortunately, this means that of his total 381 site visitors, only 123 were from his target state.

What Are Visitors Doing on Your Site?

To find out more about your visitors' behavior, navigate to "Behavior" then "Overview." This section nicely summarizes which pages are most popular with site visitors.

Unfortunately for this advisor, the data shows that very few website visitors are making it past the homepage. Only eighteen visitors made it to the blog in the last month. This is typical for an advisor without a proper marketing program in place.

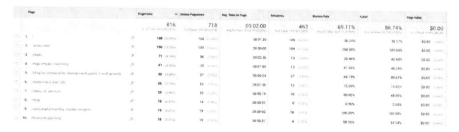

How Did Visitors Get to Your Site?

To answer this question, check out the "Acquisition" tab. This will tell you what proportion of your traffic came from each of the most common channels:

- Direct (they typed your website into their browser or clicked on a link you sent)
- Email
- Social media
- Organic search (keyword searches on Google or other search engines)
- Referrals

Google Analytics can tell a powerful story with simple information. While this advisor thought he had a successful marketing website, we can see that in reality only seven visitors from his target market in the past month actually consumed any relevant content on his website.

Armed with this information, he can adjust his marketing strategy and visit his Google Analytics again in a month or so to see whether his new strategy is working.

Does Your Site Need SEO Help?

If you're like most advisors, your email inbox is flooded with offers to improve your website's search ranking. But how do you know whether your website needs SEO work? When SEO experts tell you that your website is failing their SEO test, how can you verify this? Search engine optimization is technical and complex, but there are easy-to-use tools to identify whether your site is ranking well.

In general, your site may need SEO help if any the following are true:

- You've never done any SEO work on your site
- You have recently changed your address or phone number
- You have multiple websites or multiple firm addresses
- Your site is old, outdated, or not mobile friendly

National versus Local SEO

Before we review how to evaluate your site's SEO, let's first clarify which type of SEO you should pursue. There are two general types of SEO: national SEO (for firms such as Fidelity or Charles Schwab) and local SEO (for a specific financial advisor that belongs to one of these firms).

Google treats local businesses differently than national firms in trying to surface the best local solutions for its customers, especially for "services" categories such as "financial advisor." For this reason, it's critical to address your local, not national, SEO. This way, you'll come up for a given keyword search for people around your geographical location.

But what if you serve clients nationally? I still recommend focusing on local SEO, as trying to compete nationally is next to impossible unless you have a dedicated SEO specialist and tens of thousands of dollars per month in your budget, depending on the keywords you'd like to rank for. In my experience, even advisors who serve clients nationally are better off choosing one or two physical locations on which to focus their SEO efforts.

What Are Search Engines Looking For?

It's helpful to think of SEO in the context of the challenge that search engines face. Google, Yahoo, Bing, and others are constantly competing to return the most useful results to their users.

How can they tell whether your website is legitimate? They use clues that range from the way your site is built to the way you've registered your business to verify whether you're a credible firm. Here are some attributes that will improve your SEO score:

- A well-functioning and up-to-date website
- Mobile friendliness across devices
- Active social media profiles associated with your website
- Consistent traffic to your site
- Use of targeted keywords throughout the text and titles on your site
- Consistent address, phone number, and business name listings across directories
- Multiple verified listings for the same business location

- Local listings such as the Chamber of Commerce and Better Business Bureau
- Address listings on maps
- More than twenty identical local listings

Evaluate Your Website's Local SEO

Google may put your website into its "local search" category based on rules regarding the type of services offered, but it "knows" you are a local business if you cite other local businesses within your site. Be sure to mention and link to organizations within your community such as the Chamber of Commerce, the city you live in, volunteer organizations, and other local businesses. Also, list your street address in text on your site, not just using a map application, so the address can anchor your business as a part of local search results.

1. Check Google's Local Three Pack

The first step to evaluate the SEO score for your website is to see whether it comes up for a local search. Enter your keywords into Google along with your location name and see what Google comes up with. In this example, I used "financial advisor palm springs, ca."

Google's Local Three Pack is the top three local search results for a given term. Since most people who are evaluating service providers aim to get three quotes, it's incredibly valuable to belong to Google's Local Three Pack. The top priority of my SEO Package is to get you into these featured local listings.

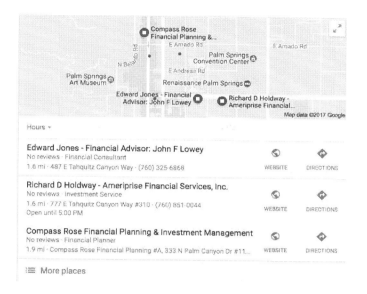

2. Search for Your Firm Name

A dead giveaway that your site has a poor SEO score is that it doesn't come up when you search for your own firm name. It's relatively easy to become the top search result for your firm name, so if you're missing the boat here, your site definitely warrants SEO work. It's important to be listed for your own name and your firm name because nine out of ten referrals will search for you on Google before they call to make an appointment. We want to make it easy to find your website, contact info, and location on a map.

3. Get Your SEO Score on WooRank.com

Woorank is an SEO and website analysis tool that can show you how your site ranks, explain what items are hurting your score, and suggest what needs to be done to improve your site. Go to woorank.com and enter your website URL. If your site has a score of 80 or less, we can improve the individual components of your SEO, including site speed, title, description, and more.

How To Optimize Your Website For Search Engines

Step 1: Make Sure Your Site Is Mobile Friendly

Recently, Google made changes to their algorithm to increase the significance of mobile-friendly sites in mobile search results. Because mobile search has now surpassed desktop search volume, this change has a large impact. Use Google's Mobile-Friendly test to make sure each page on your site passes the mobile test. If not, now is the time to make the change and upgrade to a mobile-friendly platform.

Step 2: Register Your Business with Google

Registration with Google is free and is independent of your website (though you should list your website within your business registration). Registration results in your business showing up on Google Maps and on the upper-right-hand side of the search results page, which also features your social profiles, any photos you upload, and your logo.

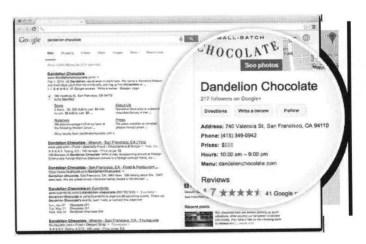

Step 3: Write Strong Title Tags and Meta Descriptions

Title tags (1) are the blue, bolded words that show up on the search engine results page. Meta descriptions (2) are the black-text words that show up underneath the title tags. Google pulls titles and descriptions from your website automatically, but that doesn't mean they represent your site well. It's important to clean up your title tags and descriptions to maximize your use of this SEO real estate. Think of these as headlines attempting to engage the viewer before they've decided whether to click on your site. Concise, well-written title tags are essential to get searchers to choose to click on your website.

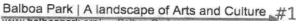

Balboa Park | A landscape of Arts and Culture #1
www.balboapark.org/ ▾ Balboa Park ▾
Information about the park's performing arts and international culture organizations, 15 museums, restaurants, zoo, gardens, hiking and biking trails and other ... #2
4.6 ★★★★★ 259 Google reviews · Write a review · Google+ page

1549 El Prado, San Diego, CA 92101
(619) 239-0512

Museums
This classic 1905 Arts and Crafts style museum home was built ...

Park Information
Welcome to Balboa Park: the nation's largest urban cultural ...

Calendar
Events - Exhibition - Organizations - Event preview. - Film - ...

Residents Free Tuesdays
Residents Free Tuesdays. As a public service, Park ...

Inside The Park
Museums - Balboa Park - Attractions - Gardens - ...

Plan Your Visit
Plan Your Visit. Balboa Park is located just minutes from ...

More results from balboapark.org »

Step 4: Write Your Keywords on Your Website

Search engines scan your website text for relevant keywords that match the keywords a potential site visitor types into the search bar. Be sure to list your business name and location within the text of your site, along with any keywords you think prospects may search for. Google can't read your company logo, so it's important to write the name of your company several times in the copy of your site. Use a keyword density tool to identify which keywords are featured on your site and their density. Aim for a keyword density of 2–5 percent for relevant words and phrases. Remember that Google gives more importance to words used in headlines and near the top of each page.

Step 5: Complete Your Business Social Media Profiles

Google gives preferential treatment to Facebook, LinkedIn, and Twitter accounts when it comes to SEO. If you have accounts on those platforms, Google will display links to your accounts on the search results page. Your goal should be to fill up the search results page and decrease the available space where competitors could appear. By adding profiles for each social site, you add search results that highlight your business. Be sure to link your social media accounts to your Google business registration to take advantage of the space where those results will be displayed.

Step 6: Consider Google AdWords

The only way to guarantee that you come up as the top result for the name of your business is to pay for that privilege. Luckily, if your site is the most relevant result for a certain search term, the price for that Google AdWord is typically low. AdWords can be a great option for advisors who are successfully embracing a niche or who do business in a smaller locality. Ads for "Financial Advisor New York" are orders of magnitude more expensive than those for "Institutional Cash Management in Fresno, California."

With pay per click (PPC) advertising, you pay the search engine (Google or Yahoo) each time someone clicks on your advertisement. The cost for each click is set by the search engine, and it depends on your location and the keywords you choose. Prices are determined by supply and demand, or how many advertisers are bidding for the specific keywords. Costs are usually correlated to location, so your price per click may be less in a small town than in a big city.

Between SEO and PPC search results, about 80 percent of users click within the SEO section, while 20 percent of users click PPC advertisements.

Since PPC is complex and changes constantly, you may choose to pay an SEO company to lower your cost per click and improve your results over time. In this scenario, you pay the SEO company directly, which then pays Google out of their institutional account and takes a percentage of your budget or a flat fee as compensation.

Goals of Paid Search for Financial Advisors

The primary goal of paid search for financial advisors is to drive more traffic to your website. Another goal is brand awareness (someone is exposed to your brand but does not visit your site). SEO improvements also add credibility, as today's consumers are used to seeing trusted brands come up prominently within search results. Another strategy for paid search is appearing for competitors' names or keywords to influence their customers.

What's the Return on Investment?

The ROI on paid search is difficult to ascertain, and SEO companies shy away from making any promises in writing. So much depends on an individual advisor's keywords, website quality, and locality that it's hard to make accurate generalizations.

That said, here is one real-life example. An advisor I work with in San Diego improved his "On-Page" SEO by working with FMG Suite to rebuild his website. Once his new site was up, he worked with FMG Suite to provide "Off-Page" SEO with the automatic social media tool. Then he worked with Google AdWords directly for PPC services.

The keywords "financial advisor san diego" were running at $2.91 per click. With a budget of $500 for the first month, he saw 171 paid clicks through to his website. Of these 171 clicks during the first month, twelve individuals filled out a form on his website. Most of them joined his newsletter mailing list, but three asked a question through his "Ask a Question" website form:

- One asked a question regarding student loan consolidation
- Another asked whether the advisor helps with LLC creation for businesses (he does not)
- Another asked about the fees the advisor charges

One promising lead called his office to set an appointment to review retirement savings.

None of these leads has converted to closed business yet. However, if we conservatively assume the value of one appointment is $1,000, the ROI for PPC would be 200% in the first month. While the quality of leads is a concern, the advisor is hopeful he'll see a meaningful long-term ROI.

The Verdict

The success of paid search will vary with each advisor, their location, and the clients they serve. Advisors in smaller localities with specific niches may see a higher return on investment.

However, as with all marketing endeavors, you are limited by how well your website converts visitors to prospects. If your website is not compelling, no amount of paid search will translate to closed business. Be sure that your website includes ways for visitors to engage short of picking up the phone. We can see from our example that calls to action like "Sign Up for Our Email Newsletter" or "Ask a Question" will get much higher participation than a call to action of "Call Now." Once you have set up a good call to action you can track your results and then work to improve both your SEO and your specific keyword performance over time.

Step 7: Hold onto Your Domain and Update Your Site Regularly

Your website's SEO will improve over time as it builds an established history, much like a credit score improves as average account ages increase. So be sure not to let your domain name registration expire.

Google likes to return websites that are timely and fresh, so rewrite the copy on your site at least once per year. Add new content and update your site at least once a month to continually improve your SEO. Weekly or monthly custom blog articles that are keyword rich are one of the best ways to accomplish this.

Think about the questions your ideal prospect may be typing into Google and answer those questions with keyword-dense blog posts to improve your SEO.

If there's one thing that's important to know about SEO, it's that it changes a lot. Be sure to stay on top of trends to keep improving your website's SEO and getting more traffic to your site.

CHAPTER 6

Create Beautiful Email Campaigns

EMAIL IS STILL the most important channel for our marketing efforts. A recent McKinsey article shows that email is forty times more effective than Facebook and Twitter combined in generating new clients. Over 90 percent of U.S. consumers check their email every day. In my work with advisors, I see roughly 70 percent of leads come from email and about 30 percent come from social media and organic search.

But success rates from email can vary widely, depending on the content and design of your campaigns. One advisor came to me with poorly designed emails and subpar results. His open rate was hovering around 13 percent and the click-through rate (how many people clicked through to read the article) was zero.

By creating more relevant content for his audience and using the tips below, over time we increased his open rate to around 40 percent. The click-through rate is now between 6 percent and 15 percent. According to data from MailChimp, the average open rate for financial emails is 21 percent and the average click-through rate is 2.76 percent, so our rates are about double the industry standard.

The first step to designing and sending great emails is to use an email marketing software to create and schedule your emails so you can include images and branding.

Step 1: Choose Your Email Marketing Service – Mailchimp or Constant Contact

With all the email marketing software available, how can advisors be sure to choose the best option? Let's review why we want to use email marketing software in the first place:

- Since more emails are opened today on iPhones than desktops, you'll want your email to look great on every device.
- When sending to a list of contacts, you will want to keep track of open rates, click-through rates, and unsubscribe rates so you can do more of what works.
- Using graphics in our emails increases our click-through rates, so we'll want to include a clickable graphic.
- A/B testing allows us to test alternate subject lines, graphics, and email design to improve the performance of our marketing.
- Email software systems archive all campaigns as a backup for compliance.
- Built-in footers and unsubscribe links comply with federal spam laws.

The two platforms most commonly used by financial advisors are Constant Contact and MailChimp. Which one is right for you? Here's how they measure up.

First, a Little Background

Constant Contact is an email marketing behemoth founded in 1995 in Waltham, Massachusetts. They have more than 1,200 employees around the country and went public in 2007. At over 20 years old they are a great-grandfather by Internet standards, and they have been criticized for being a Web 1.0 company trying to compete in a Web 2.0 world.

MailChimp was founded in 2001 in Atlanta, Georgia, and currently has about 500 employees. The company is privately held, which they claim helps them "work quickly and respond to technology changes without anything getting in their way." With a decidedly tech-savvy company culture, MailChimp advertises via popular podcasts to younger business leaders and startups.

Email Design

Let's compare the look and feel of emails between the two systems. Here's the same email created with Constant Contact (top) and MailChimp (bottom):

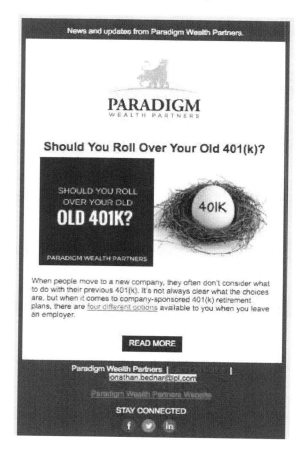

The MailChimp version appears a little more modern, less cluttered, and more aesthetically pleasing. MailChimp has more leeway and functionality to make an email look great. As a marketer, that alone is enough to sway my preference.

Ease of Use

If you've been using Constant Contact and are comfortable with it, there's no reason to make the switch for ease of use. But if you're starting fresh and aim to make life easy, consider MailChimp. The software review company Capterra studied which platform business owners preferred. Of users who had tried both platforms, 75 percent preferred MailChimp. My personal preference from an ease-of-use perspective is MailChimp by an order of magnitude.

System Speed

The biggest downside for me of Constant Contact is that their system is painstakingly slow. It's like going back to 1994 to use the Internet. Editing an email, making changes to your contact list, or viewing reports takes ten times longer than with MailChimp.

Each time I click on a button within Constant Contact, it takes 5–7 full seconds to load the next page. MailChimp takes less than a second. This may not matter much if you're only sending out one email per month, but because I send dozens of emails per day on behalf of my clients, these precious seconds add up.

Deliverability

Published deliverability rates, or what percentage of your emails get through to a recipient's inbox, are about the same: Constant Contact claims a 98 percent delivery rate and MailChimp claims 96–99 percent. But what about in real life?

I sent an email to the exact same contact list via MailChimp and Constant Contact. The MailChimp email had a 100 percent successful delivery rate, with a 47 percent open rate and a 25 percent click-through rate. The Constant Contact email had a 99 percent delivery rate, with just one email bounce. But the open rate was 31 percent and the click-through rate was 16 percent. MailChimp is the clear winner.

Unsubscribing

MailChimp has a one-click unsubscribe feature, while Constant Contact has a two-step process. This may not seem like a big deal, but in email marketing, we strive to make unsubscribing as easy as possible to avoid spam complaints.

Unsubscribes are a normal, healthy part of email marketing. Spam complaints are not and can trigger restrictions on your ability to send emails successfully. If it's difficult for a recipient to unsubscribe, they may click the spam button, which is to be avoided at all costs.

Customer Support

Constant Contact has customer support by email and phone, so they are technically the winner in this category. But MailChimp is easier to use and has a monkey at the top of each page offering you helpful tips, so if you don't mind online and email support, MailChimp has plenty of resources available.

Pricing

MailChimp is free for up to 2,000 subscribers, which will cover the average financial advisor. Constant Contact starts at $20 per month and requires users to pay $5 extra per month to host images for emails.

Reporting

Reporting is essential to understand how your emails are performing and to compare results across campaigns. Constant Contact reporting is crude at best, with a table displaying the results of each campaign:

	Time Sent	Campaign Name	Total Sent	Open Rate	Click Through Rate	Bounce Rate	Unsubscribe Rate
☐	Tue, Jun 14, 2016 6:00 AM	Should You Roll Over Your Old 401(k)?	210	15.8% 33	9.1% 2	0.5% 1	1% 2
☐	Wed, Jun 1, 2016 11:07 AM	Did You Know Paradigm Wealth Partners Runs on Referrals?	210	31.6% 66	16.7% 11	0.5% 1	0% 0

MailChimp has robust reporting, with graphical representations of email campaign performance over time. It provides more data for individual campaigns, including when your contacts are opening and clicking on your emails.

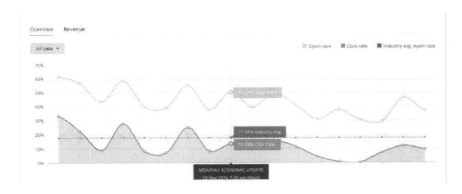

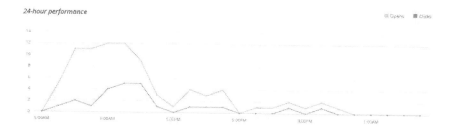

A/B Testing

A/B testing allows you to test variations of your email on a small group of your contacts, then send the "winning" version to your entire contact list. Testing can significantly improve the performance of emails and is critical to a professional marketing strategy.

This is where Constant Contact really fails, with no built-in A/B testing. You have to build and run a test manually, which can get messy and risks duplicate emails being sent to some recipients.

MailChimp offers automatic A/B testing, even with their free account. You select which variable you'd like to test, what percentage of your overall list you'd like to use as a test pool, and how long the system should wait before selecting a winner and sending it to the remainder of your list. In one experiment I conducted, an A/B test for a subject line doubled the email open rate and quadrupled the click-through rate.

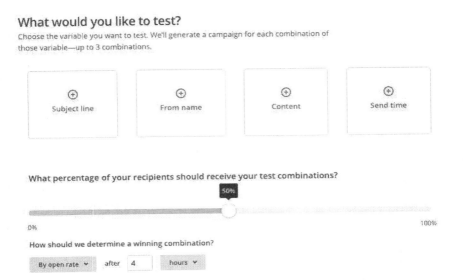

Compliance

If your firm is an RIA or you are with a major independent broker-dealer other than LPL Financial, you can choose between the two platforms. (Be sure to check this with your broker-dealer first.) If you are with LPL Financial, as many of my clients are, you will not be able to use MailChimp at this time. Despite its having the same functionality and compliance archiving capabilities as Constant Contact, LPL has not approved MailChimp yet.

Overall, MailChimp is the clear winner in my tests and among users. If your compliance department allows it, MailChimp is an easy-to-use and cost-effective email marketing platform. If not, Constant Contact is an adequate alternative until your compliance department updates their stance in the future.

Step 2: Build Your Email List with Friends and Family

When I work with advisors to build their email lists, they often ask whether they should add friends and family. While I never advocate "selling" via relatives and social acquaintances, there are two solid reasons to add your personal contacts to your email list today.

Help Prospects Find You When They Need You Most

The type of content marketing strategy I run for advisors is designed not to sell, but to help people find them *when they need them most*. If your network doesn't understand what you do and who you help, they can't refer business to you. I coach advisors to make their niche so clear that *even those who don't buy can still refer.*

Family, friends, neighbors, and acquaintances are great referral sources if they understand what your niche is. If you share your newsletter with them, they'll better understand what you do and how you can help. In turn, they will be able to help people find you when they need you most.

Your referral pipeline is strengthened when conversations with family or neighbors go from "I think Tom is in finance" to "Tom helps divorcing spouses get a fair and equitable settlement" or "My brother-in-law helps Baby Boomers who own a business catch up on their retirement savings in a hurry."

Improve Deliverability of Your Emails

Take a look at this case study analyzing the difference in email behavior of friends and family vs. business contacts. I uploaded business contacts and personal contacts for one of my advisors and did a simple A/B test. The open rate for business contacts was 21.7 percent, which isn't too shabby.

		603 Subscribers	21.7% Opens	2.2% Clicks
✓	Should You Swap Your Life Insurance for Long-Term Care Insurance? Regular · LinkedIn Connections Sent on Tue, Dec 29, 2015 07:00 am			

However, the open rate for friends and family was 48 percent, which is phenomenal. By combining the two lists, we increase the average for the overall list.

		53 Subscribers	48.0% Opens	14.0% Clicks
✓	Will Your Inheritance be a Gift or a Curse? Regular · Prospects Sent on Fri, Nov 06, 2015 11:30 am			

This is important because how well your emails get delivered depends on both open rate and click-through rate. For this reason, we want to send to folks who know our name and will open our emails. And we want to include one clear call to action for them to click on.

Many advisors put the whole blog post or article in the body of an email, but that doesn't drive traffic to their website for conversion. If you have a low click-through rate, your emails are more likely to be seen as spam and less likely to be delivered by mail delivery systems.

You may be wary of adding friends and family to your email list, but I promise people who care about you want to know what you're up to (Hi, Mom!). If you're offering truly original, helpful, and interesting content, they'll appreciate your emails even more.

Step 3: Work with Compliance

In reality, most advisors have been blogging for years; they just don't know it. A blog consists of pieces of copy called "posts." Each post is a short article that you've authored and placed on your website. Like any article, it must go through Compliance before distribution to the public. If you have been writing your own correspondence for use with clients, the rules for blogging won't be any different:

Don't Get Specific

It's impossible to know the unique situation of every person who reads your post, so you can't know which investments would be appropriate for them. Stick to describing a product or the situation in which considering a certain investment would be appropriate.

Do Get Personal

Many advisors are hesitant to share personal information because they believe clients will find it uninteresting or irrelevant. However, relating a personal story to an everyday financial issue that many people face is a great way to explain a concept or service. Given how dry financial advice can sometimes be, weaving a story makes the issue human and helps clients make the connection to something they understand personally.

Bring out the Buffers

You likely already know that Compliance won't allow promissory language such as "I create a financial plan that achieves your goals," but that doesn't mean you need to avoid explaining the benefits you offer your clients. Add a few buffer words to your statements, such as "I create a financial plan designed to lead you on a path toward your goals." Other buffer words that help to keep your words from sounding too promissory are: "My goal is to…," "I am committed to…," "We aim/seek/strive to…," "I help clients pursue…," "Strategies I create…" If you're unclear about this, reach out to your compliance officer to determine which wording will be acceptable.

Sorry, No Comment

Because you can't control what a visitor might say in a comment on your website, broker-dealers typically require you to disable commenting. Instead, invite readers to connect with you directly and continue the conversation one-on-one by email.

Disclose, Disclose, Disclose

Your broker-dealer may require you to use disclosures on your blog just as you do on your website. For example, if you mention certain services or specific advisors, you may need to include a disclosure at the end.

Play by Your Rules

This may seem obvious, but many advisors forget that different broker-dealers have different rules about what they do or don't allow. Just because you hear a fellow advisor with another broker-dealer say something isn't allowed, it doesn't necessarily mean that's true for your home office. Review the rules before you start writing. You'll get better at sticking to them as you practice, and in time you may not need to refer to the rules to know whether what you're writing will be approved.

Step 4: Craft a Perfect Marketing Email

Only One Topic Per Email

Probably the most common mistake advisors make, in an effort to send fewer emails or to make their newsletters seem more valuable, is to pack a hodge-podge of information into a cluttered email design.

Multi-topic newsletters are ineffective for two reasons. First, with no clear action to take, readers are paralyzed by too many options and give up. Second, even if readers are interested in your content, they'll put the multi-subject email aside to read when they have time, which is a day that never comes.

With one topic per email, you capture the reader's attention, give them one (and only one) next step to take, and allow them to fully consume your content so they feel educated and empowered. This creates a more fulfilling experience, which inspires them to open more of your emails in the future. It's also easier to forward an email with just one topic since the forwarder doesn't have to clarify which article they felt was of interest. You're much better off sending weekly one-topic emails than a monthly newsletter of chaos.

The Sender Is Someone the Recipient Knows

Your emails should never be sent from your firm's name, Admin, or info@ xyzfinancial.com. They should come from you, as the author of the post. MailChimp lets you upload your headshot, so recipients may see your photo, depending on which email client they use. I like to add credentials and the firm name too, so it's clear exactly who you are.

Preheader Text Gives Context

Depending on your recipient's email client (Google, Outlook, etc.), the pre-header text may be visible in their inbox. Make sure it's customized to give some context, such as "News and Financial Updates from XYZ Financial." For bonus points, customize the preheader for each email to make it relevant. Be sure it includes a link to view the email in their browser in case the recipient's email security filters do not allow your images to be displayed. MailChimp automatically populates this for you.

The Logo Header Links to Your Homepage

The header of the email is your branding, identifying your firm. Clicking on your logo should take the recipient to your homepage, where they can reacquaint themselves with who you are and what you do.

Craft a Captivating Subject Line

Good subject lines are critical for getting recipients to open your email and click on the information you've sent. Luckily, this aspect of marketing, which used to be an art, is now a science that we can measure, test, and track.

Many advisors spend hours creating a great marketing email, then type the subject as an afterthought. The example below shows how a captivating subject line can make or break your email campaign. For this A/B test, a change in only the subject line *doubled* the email open rate and *quadrupled* the clicks through to the content.

The first subject line ("What's New from Indigo Marketing?") generated just under 15 percent opens and 12.5 percent clicks. The improved subject line ("What Is Harry Markowitz Doing Today? And More from Indigo Marketing") provided just under 30 percent opens and 25 percent clicks. With an email list of 500 recipients, that's the difference between 62 and 125 website visits.

Write a Winning Subject Line

Writing a subject line that converts is both an art and a science. I start by writing subject lines that include some of the words that years of research has shown to convert powerfully:

- You
- Your
- How
- New
- Make
- Know

It's not as hard as you would think to include several of these words in one subject line. My first impulse, "How to Double Your Email ROI with a Better Subject Line," includes two of these high-converting words.

Score Your Subject Line

Next, I use Coschedule.com's scoring technology to improve the subject line to a score of 65 or greater. My two test lines were "Think Your Email Subject Line Doesn't Matter? Think Again," which scored 65, and "How to Double Your Email ROI with a Better Subject Line," which scored 78.

Run an A/B Test

Once I have two options that I'm confident in, I run a real email A/B test. My email goes out to the first 10 percent of my email list in two groups, one with subject A and one with subject B. The winning subject line goes out to the remaining 90 percent of my list.

Harnessing Science

Turning our marketing from an art into a science and testing the results can create big improvements in our conversion rates. The impact is even greater for advisors with large networks and email lists. For my advisor clients who send emails to more than 1,000 recipients, I recommend testing at least four subject lines to find the one that converts the most leads.

One of my advisor clients has an opportunity to send an email to 50,000 members of a professional group he serves. We'll be testing four email and subject variations in advance of the send to double the leads he'll receive from the campaign.

Add a Relevant Graphic

According to HubSpot, emails with relevant images get 94 percent more views than those without. Make sure that your image is clickable and links to your article.

I am always amazed to see emails or blog posts that feature unrelated, irrelevant graphics. On my first day of business school, a notoriously tough professor began teaching his course with his first slide featuring only a thumbs-up sign. He said that if we ever included an irrelevant graphic in a presentation, he would immediately fail us. I guess that's where my pet peeve came from.

Choose a consistent them for your email graphics – for example, black-and-white photography or the same branded overlay. We use Canva.com to design graphics for each of the advisors we work with to tell a consistent story. The first post below was sent to physicians, so it features a doctor working with a patient. The second post is about retirement planning, so it features a retired couple. Both are in line with the advisor's overall branding, so they offer a cohesive experience.

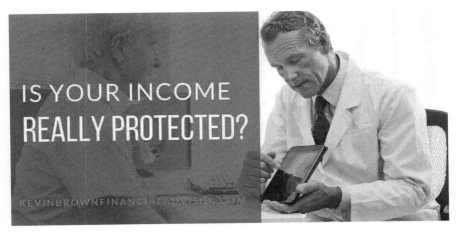

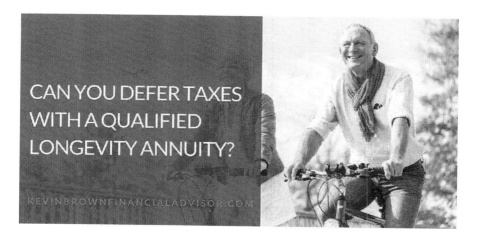

Teaser Text Invites Readers to Learn More

Your teaser text appears in the body of your email, below the graphic and above the call to action button. It should be an adapted introduction to your article that piques interest and offers a link for readers to learn more. Here's one example:

> When we face life's tough decisions, such as a career move or a medical treatment, we usually conduct research and gather information. Sometimes we look to trusted experts or even the Internet to get a second opinion. But what about your financial plan? Does it deserve a second opinion?

Include a Button Call to Action

Always include a clear, clickable button that screams "click me" linking to your blog post. The text that appears on the button will depend on the content of your email:

- Learn More
- Get Started
- See Photos
- Watch Video
- Register Now

Now your email will have three separate links that readers can click on to learn more: the graphic, the teaser text, and the button.

Include Social Media Buttons

Include buttons for your website and all of your social media profiles so the recipient can connect with you on their preferred platform to stay in touch.

Make Your Footer Discreet

There's no need to disrupt the reading experience by interjecting disclosures within the body of your email. Put your disclosures and information required by spam law in the footer of your email. MailChimp automatically includes your physical address and a link to unsubscribe, which are both required by federal spam regulations.

Now that you've designed your perfect marketing email, how often should you send it? Data from MailChimp shows that unsubscribe rates don't increase significantly when you go from sending emails once per month to once per week. However, unsubscribes do go up substantially when you email more often.

Step 5: Write Your Most Important Email Ever

There's one quick and easy post you can write that typically gets twice as many views as any other type: explaining why you do what you do. The concept is highlighted in Simon Sinek's book *Start with Why*. This is always the top-performing blog post for the advisors I work with. To get started, answer the following questions:

- Why did you get into this business?
- Why did you become an independent advisor?
- What's the most important thing you provide to clients?
- Why do your clients choose to work with you instead of someone else?
- What's the most difficult part of your job?

- What's the most fulfilling part of your job?
- When was one time you knew you had made a difference?
- What do you most hope to offer your clients?

Write a 300–600-word blog post telling your story to kick off your content marketing journey!

Email Best Practices and Bonus Tips

1. Schedule Your Emails for Success

The best time to send an email depends on your particular network. I always get a kick out of seeing the peak days and times for different industries. For divorce lawyers, most website activity happens at 11 p.m. on Thursday nights (after a long week and a fight, presumably). Nanny providers have the most searches at 11 a.m. Monday mornings (when the kids finally go down for a nap after a long weekend). For the advisors I work with, I run a report using Google Analytics to determine when their particular network is most active; then we schedule their marketing emails at this time.

Day of Week Name	Users
	1,089
	% of Total: 100.00% (1,089)
1. Tuesday	**266** (20.31%)
2. Thursday	**221** (16.87%)
3. Wednesday	**200** (15.27%)
4. Friday	**185** (14.12%)
5. Sunday	**177** (13.51%)
6. Monday	**147** (11.22%)
7. Saturday	**114** (8.70%)

2. Offer Different Calls to Action

You'll notice that at the end of my emails and blog posts, I give the reader a few options to take the next step toward working with me:

Want to bring your email marketing up to speed? Visit my website to learn more about what I do or schedule a virtual meeting to discuss your business. Not ready to double your leads with email marketing? Stay in touch by connecting with me on LinkedIn and signing up for my marketing newsletter.

I recommend offering choices so that readers at different engagement levels can find an appropriate next step to take with your firm. Examples include options to read more about this topic, watch a related video, ask a question, sign up for our newsletter, register for a webinar, sign up for an event, schedule an appointment, or call our office.

3. Segment Your List

Segment your contact list and send relevant information to each group. For advisors, I recommend segmenting into age groups of 35–59 and 60+ at the very least. I also recommend segmenting by birthday month so you can deliver one message each month to clients with birthdays. Using a CRM system such as Redtail makes this a snap. While some content will be relevant for many groups, you should attempt to craft your marketing to be specific to one group at a time.

4. Send Regular Emails

This may be obvious, but it takes more than one email to build a relationship with a prospect. Sending regular marketing emails with valuable information builds your relationship and keeps you on the top of their mind. It's important to send emails at a regular cadence to establish consistency. Research shows that unsubscribe rates go up when emails are increased to once per month, but do not increase again until they are sent more than once per week. For this reason, I recommend sending emails at least twice a month, and ideally once a week.

5. Track Your Success

Email marketing engines allow you to easily track how your campaigns are working. For each campaign, I run a report to see how many opens, clicks, and forwards the email produced. I track these numbers over time so we can make a note of the topics that each audience segment enjoys and keep tabs on overall progress.

If you can commit to one marketing activity to increase your leads, I recommend bi-weekly email marketing. While email marketing is incredibly effective, it can be time-consuming. A Constant Contact survey of small business owners estimated that getting an extra hour in their day back from doing their own email marketing is worth $273. By working with a marketing consultant to automate the process, you can set a schedule for consistent email marketing that pays off over time.

Step 6: Optimize Your Email Content for Your Blog

Showing up for keyword searches helps people find you when they need your help. But there's a lot of competition for hot keywords, and SEO isn't as straightforward as it used to be. Here's what you can do today to get your blog posts to show up for specific Google searches.

The Right Length

A blog post that is shorter than 300 words won't help your SEO. Why? First, it's difficult to maximize your keywords in such a limited space. Ideally, you should include your keywords multiple times in your blog post. But if your article is only a few hundred words long, you don't have the space to include those keywords more than once or twice. Second, Google and other search engines are looking for content in order to rank your website. A number of studies show that more text correlates with higher search engine rankings.

A blog post that is between 500 and 1,000 words is long enough to capture several keywords and other SEO-friendly elements, but not so long that it becomes overwhelming for your visitor to read. According to Medium, the optimal blog post (in terms of number of views) takes 3–7 minutes to read. Above the 7-minute mark, readers start to drop off and leave the page, and if your audience is not reading your entire article, they could be missing the critical concluding remarks and your call to action.

Make Your Important Statements First

While we all enjoy a little mystery in life, an SEO-friendly blog post is more documentary than murder mystery. Rather than having a lengthy introduction relaying a story that leads up to your key point, work backwards. Make your most important points first. Start with a powerful statement (with punchy keywords, of course) and then dive into your personal story or other details you want to incorporate.

Understand the Role of Google

Google aim to be the best search engine, which means they want to deliver the most relevant results. Google judge how helpful their results are by how long visitors stay on a website, how much of a blog post they read, and whether they click through to other content on the site. They also consider website credibility indicators such as the total traffic to a website, how many other websites link to that site, and whether the site is connected to active social media profiles.

All of these factors give Google a glimpse into how legitimate and helpful a website is. Their algorithm for determining which results to return for a given keyword search is constantly being updated to make their search engine better. No one knows exactly how it works, and SEO experts are constantly trying to play catch-up.

Create Valuable Blog Posts

In the old days, you could stuff keywords into your website so that Google would think your site was highly relevant to a specific topic. This meant you could put "Financial Planning" over and over on the pages of your site to show up for that keyword search. Google got wise, and now "keyword stuffing" is actually penalized.

Google calculates your keyword density, or the number of times a keyword is used divided by the total words on the page. If your keyword density is too high, your post will be punished by the Google gods.

The only way to show up in search results today is to create valuable and helpful content. Google knows whether your content is helpful by watching the behavior of people who search for something and end up on your site.

Answering a question well and keeping people on your site longer can help your blog posts rank higher in search results. My blog post "Ten Secrets to Promoting Your Event" is one of the highest-ranked posts on my site because it thoroughly answers a common search question about how best to promote an event online.

Focus on Only One or Two Keywords

In each blog post, focus on one or two keywords to write about. It could be "key person life insurance" or "ETF investing." By targeting your content to specific keywords, you're more likely to come up in those searches.

Once you choose they keywords you'd like to focus on, it's important to use them in the right areas of your post. Google gives hierarchical credibility to your post's title, headings, and URL, so use your keywords in these three places.

Add a Meta Description

A meta description is a 160-character-or-less summary of your blog post. The meta description shows up below the title of your post in search results. It's important to create an accurate meta description so that Google knows what the post is about and people will click on your post in their search results. Most website platforms for advisors have an area to add a meta description. If you have a WordPress site, you can use the Yoast SEO plugin to optimize your meta description.

Make Sure Your Blog Is Mobile Friendly

Because the majority of website traffic comes from mobile devices today, Google will penalize sites that are not mobile friendly because they don't provide a good user experience.

Optimize Your Images

Like my business school professor, Google likes relevant imagery. They prefer that you use a relevant image and label it appropriately by providing "alt-text." Screen readers used by blind and visually impaired people depend on images being labeled properly in this way, and adding an accurate label to your images improves your SEO score.

Create a Lot of Content on the Same Topic

I wish there were shortcuts to mastering search engine optimization, but there aren't. The best way to be seen as credible and helpful by Google is to create a lot of great content on your specialty.

One of my clients does this as well as anyone. Steven H. Kobrin, LUTCF, is also known as the life insurance guru. His blog posts cover everything you'd ever want to know about life insurance, including posts such as:

- The Guide to Buying Life Insurance (eBook)
- How Business Owners Use Life Insurance to Fund Buy-Sell Agreements
- Get Life Insurance If You're a Cancer Survivor
- How to Evaluate the Credentials of Your Life Insurance Broker
- Will Your Life Insurance Cover Your Emotional Needs?
- Should Your Children Be Your Life Insurance Beneficiary?
- Premium Financing for Life Insurance
- The Blunt Truth About Marijuana and Life Insurance

Steve does an incredible job covering this topic. Each blog post you create on the same topic adds to your site's SEO credibility.

Link to Your Related Blog Posts

Remember how Google judges how helpful your site is by how long someone is on your site and whether they click through to your other content? That's where internal linking comes in. You'll want to link to your other blog posts on related topics to give readers helpful information and keep them on your site longer. Aim for at least three internal links per post.

Get Others to Link to Your Post

Getting other websites to link to your site, or "backlinking," used to be the biggest trick in the SEO book. But then SEO specialists spent their time adding links to their clients' posts in the comments section of other websites and Google got wise.

Today, backlinking isn't as powerful as it used to be, but having other credible sites link to your post will help your SEO. Publish your posts on related sites, share them with professional partners, and let key influencers know about your content. Every time an industry leader such as Michael Kitces links to one of my blog posts, that post gets a big SEO boost.

Share by Email and Social Media

If you found an incredibly valuable blog post on a topic that interested you, what's the first thing you would do? You'd share it via email or on social media. A lot of shares gives Google a big clue that your post is valuable. Share each of your blog posts with everyone in your network by email and on social media.

CHAPTER 7

Create a Rock-Solid Social Media Presence

IF THERE IS one thing I encounter over and over with the advisors I work with, it's their too-strong-for-reason resistance to joining social media.

A social media presence has been proven to be an important component of an effective marketing plan, so why is there still strong opposition? Here are my top theories for why almost half of advisors are not yet tweeting, posting, and liking their way to new business:

No Instant Gratification

We all love instant gratification. That's why we gamble (even though we know we're likely placing a losing bet) and eat that second scoop of ice cream. It's tough to stick to a plan that doesn't pay off right away. But as the Latin phrase "gutta cavat lapidem" ("a water drop hollows a stone") suggests, progress is sometimes made not by force but by small actions repeated often.

Social media pays off at its own pace, but when it does, the payoff tends to be significant. Take the recent example of a San Diego advisor who had been using social media for 6 months with no results, until a college sorority sister Facebook messaged her that she had just inherited $2 million from her grandmother. The payoff might be delayed and unpredictable, but you can't afford to miss out.

It's Confusing

The digital age has changed our lives at an alarming rate, and those of us who don't consider ourselves tech-savvy have had a hard time keeping up. Social media and its terminology can be confusing, overwhelming, and downright annoying. But the fundamentals are very simple: *LinkedIn is a place to connect with professionals. Twitter is a place to share content. Facebook is a place to connect with friends. YouTube is a place to share videos.*

If you don't "get" social media, the best way to understand is to try it out by spending some time on the most popular sites. There are good reasons social media websites dominate traffic on the Internet: they're fun and interesting to use. Enlist your tech-savvy spouse, child, or friend to explain the basics and help you set up an account, and then explore at your own pace to find out what all the hype is about.

Compliance Fears

The most common explanation (or excuse) I hear from advisors is that compliance regulations keep them from joining social media. Sure, compliance can be a burden, but the same rules apply whether you are writing a letter to clients, creating collaterals for a seminar, or posting to social media. You must follow basic guidelines and avoid promissory statements. Broker-dealer firms have come a long way in recent years to support and facilitate advisors' use of social media.

The key point to understand is that the nature of social media marketing is not to make specific recommendations, but to offer general information and entertaining articles and videos, and to connect with clients on a personal level. Compliance will not stand in the way of your using social media to achieve these results.

It Takes Too Much Time

Having a polished, professional, and engaging social media presence does take some time. But the truth is that your social media efforts can and should coincide with the work you put into being a great advisor. All good advisors read interesting articles, watch educational videos, and come across compelling data. Take a few extra moments to share this information with your network and you've got a great social media presence. Clients appreciate when you share valuable information with them – whether it's about a new tax law, an interesting data point, or a local charity golf tournament. Invest a few extra minutes to post content you already consume and you will engage clients and prospects in a whole new way.

The Cost

To be fair, there are often monetary costs associated with social media and compliance mechanisms to track them. However, these costs are relatively small and generally decreasing, as broker-dealers continue to recognize the importance of social media marketing for advisors. It's important to look at these costs as a fraction of your total marketing budget, similar to the postage for a direct mail campaign. If you get one new client or ten good ideas from the endeavor, these costs have been covered. Envision the price as an investment in future business and let it be a motivation to regularly use you social media accounts.

Still hesitant to get started? What's your excuse? Social media accounts only take a few minutes to set up and less than 10 minutes a day to keep current. Don't worry if you miss a day or two. As long as you have an account and post every once in a while, it counts as "being on social media." Give it a few months, keep sharing interesting content, and be patient; a water drop hollows a stone.

Step 1: LinkedIn

You may have a LinkedIn profile, but do you also have a LinkedIn Company Page for your business? While your LinkedIn profile showcases you, a company page showcases your company. It's like a profile for your firm. Anyone can follow your company page to see your updates, you can post job listings from the page, and your employees can list your company as their employer in their profiles.

We create and optimize the LinkedIn Company Page for financial advisors to round out their social media presence and improve their exposure online.

Benefits of a LinkedIn Company Page

- A company page allows you to enter information about your firm on LinkedIn so that people can find it.

- Your logo and company name appear next to your "Current Position" on your profile.

- Your employees can also be associated with your firm through their current position. When people click on your firm, they can see everyone who works there.

- Perhaps most importantly, a company page improves your website's SEO. By listing your company name, address, and website, you give search engines another point of credibility to legitimize your business online.

- If you're a large firm, you can create a careers section and post jobs through the company page.

- When you share content from your company page, everyone who follows your page will see your posts.

How to Set Up and Optimize Your LinkedIn Company Page

Follow these steps to set up your LinkedIn Company Page:

1. Select "Work" in the top toolbar, scroll down to "Create A Company Page +" and click the link.

2. Enter your full business name. If the name is already taken as a company page URL, copy your company website URL or your Twitter username. LinkedIn will warn you if another page has the same name. Click to review these other pages to avoid creating a duplicate page.

3. Once you have created the page, click "Manage" then "Overview" to make the following updates:

   - "Update Profile Picture" with your business logo. Make sure to use a square image file so it appears correctly, at least 400 × 400 pixels for good image clarity.

   - "Update Cover Image." Make sure the image you choose is at least 1536 × 768 pixels. Only a small portion of the height will be shown, so don't use an image that needs to be completely visible to make sense.

- "Update About Us" section with your current company bio or mission statement. Add disclosures to the bottom of this section if required.

- Add your company URL and fill in the required fields that follow.

- Add your company address.

4. When you are done, click "Go to Member View" and select "Publish." Review the full page and make any necessary adjustments.

5. Go to your personal LinkedIn profile and make sure the company logo is visible under your "Experience" section. If not, edit your current position, enter the company name again, and select the company page from the dropdown suggestions.

6. Revisit this process annually to make sure the summaries and contact info are up to date.

Being successful on LinkedIn is a lot like staying fit. It works best if you put a few minutes toward your efforts on a regular basis, not all at once. I recommend spending your first cup of coffee at the office on LinkedIn. Here's what to do:

Connect with Everyone You Meet

The first step of strengthening your online networking muscles is to always work toward expanding your network. Be sure to connect with all your clients, not just your top clients, as well as everyone you meet while networking or socializing. The larger your network, the more opportunities you have to find qualified prospects. My rule of thumb for who to connect with is anyone you have met in person, worked with virtually, or would feel comfortable introducing to someone else in your network.

Reach Out to Referral Partners

Spend some time each week to reach out to CPAs, estate planning attorneys, lawyers, real estate agents, and other potential referral partners. Send a brief message introducing yourself and explaining who you work with and how you can help. Ask about their own specialty to understand what they do best.

Seek Out Centers of Influence

Centers of influence, or COIs, are the movers and shakers in your locality: the mayor, top business leaders, the lady who works at the coffee cart and has her finger on the pulse of your town. Make sure these folks know exactly what you do so they can introduce you to others and share your information. One way to help them understand your firm is to invite them in for a "mock client meeting" so they get an introduction to your philosophy, your process, and your team.

Share Valuable Content

Content is at the core of our LinkedIn strategy. Use the content from your email campaigns and blog as a starting point. Each day, you'll want to spend a minute or two sharing content that your network will find valuable.

Respond to All Messages

The etiquette for responding to Facebook messages is about 24 hours, 48 hours for LinkedIn, and only 2 hours for Twitter messages. For this reason, I caution advisors from pursuing a Twitter-centric strategy unless they can commit to quick responses every day. To demonstrate good LinkedIn manners, be sure to check and respond to your messages on at least Monday, Wednesday, and Friday.

Engage with Others

Engaging with others shows that you are interested in what they're doing. Read their articles, "like" their posts, and comment on their discussions. This also helps you understand what your clients and prospects are consuming and sharing online, which is helpful when you create your custom content strategy.

Discuss within Groups

LinkedIn groups are powerful because they allow you to interact with people you don't know. Spend some time perusing the discussions within your groups, sharing content, and offering your two cents' worth. I recently landed a big speaking engagement after an industry leader read a blog post I shared in a group we both belong to. Don't limit your groups to business; have some fun discussing your passions in groups of like-minded enthusiasts. One of my clients spends his time chatting in LinkedIn classic car groups.

Follow Key Influencers

One of my advisors likes to say, "I've never had a new idea in my life, so if you steal from me, you're stealing twice." Following key influencers is an excellent opportunity to learn what top networkers are doing and to copy what works. You can follow people without being connected to them by clicking the "Follow" button on the dropdown menu next to "Connect." You can also get exposure by liking and commenting on key influencers' content, because other folks in their network will see your activity.

Browse the News

Your LinkedIn newsfeed is a great place to read articles, see what people are sharing, and watch videos. It's not designed for breaking news, but there is a treasure trove of specific, insightful content that experts in your network publish directly to LinkedIn.

Make Introductions

You can introduce two people in your LinkedIn network by going to one contact's profile, clicking on the dropdown next to "Message," and selecting "Share." This sends a message offering to introduce the recipient to the contact you shared. This feature is great for helping someone in your network with a job search or introducing two business colleagues. The downside is that both folks have to be relatively proficient with LinkedIn, so I use the feature only when I'm sure they are pretty active on the site.

Take the LinkedIn marketing challenge and commit to spending 10 minutes each weekday on LinkedIn for 6 months! The advisors I work with report increased connections, referrals, and new clients as a result. If you'd like to learn a lot more about how to use LinkedIn to reach qualified prospects, check out my book *The LinkedIn Guide for Financial Advisors* on Amazon.

Step 2: Don't Underestimate Facebook

The best time to set up a Facebook Business Page for your financial planning firm is a year ago or today. While it may seem like a frivolous diversion of resources in the short term, the fact is that using a Facebook Business Page is the only way for advisors to:

- Target prospects based on zip code, age, and interests
- Gain daily exposure to your clients and their friends
- Tag clients in event photos to get exposure to their network
- Get listed on the pages of nearby businesses
- List your business on Facebook maps

Users Spend 50 Minutes Per Day on Facebook

The popularity of Facebook means it can be more powerful than LinkedIn and Twitter. There's a good reason Facebook calls its members "users": they seem to be truly addicted. The *New York Times* reported in May 2016 that the average user spends 50 minutes per day on the site and logs on every single day – and twice on weekends.

While Facebook is only one piece of the larger marketing puzzle and can be slow to get off the ground, my clients who have been sending content out for at least 6 months have had the following successes:

- 40–100 website visits per month from Facebook
- Hundreds of clients and prospects following their business page
- Exposure to 300 or more prospects for each post on Facebook

Claiming your business page will also improve the SEO of your business website. Despite the power of Facebook, many advisors resist creating a business page because they don't understand how to execute a professional business marketing strategy on a site full of baby photos and cat videos.

It's important to understand that a Facebook Business Page is not a personal profile. Personal profiles have "friends," while business pages have "likes." Although a business page must be created from a personal profile, you do not need to be active on your personal profile to have a business page.

Some advisors confuse their Facebook feed (where they see the personal posts of their friends) with their Facebook Business Page (where only the page administrator can approve posts). With the correct settings, the casual nature of Facebook will not dilute the professionalism of your firm, because you get to approve all posts on your page in advance.

How to Set Up Your Facebook Business Page

Facebook requires that a business page to be set up from a personal Facebook profile. If you don't have a Facebook account, sign up or have someone in your office use their Facebook profile to set up the page:

1. Once you log into Facebook, click on the arrow in the top-right corner to drop down the menu and choose "Create Page."

2. Choose a business category for your page. I recommend "Local Business."

3. Choose an industry-specific category. I recommend "Licensed Financial Representative."

4. Enter your business address so you are listed on Facebook maps and people can "Check In" at your office.

5. Add a short description of your firm and your website URL.

6. Add a photo of you, your team, or your firm's logo as the profile photo.

7. Create a unique username of the form www.facebook.com/yourfirmname.

8. Add your page to your favorites on your Facebook account. This will give you easy access to it when you log in.

9. Add a long description of your firm and include disclosures.

10. Adjust your settings to require post approval by the administrator. Go to "Settings," then "Visitor Posts," and check the box next to "Review Posts Before They Are Published To Page."

11. Add a background image that relates to your firm or location.

12. Submit to Compliance for approval.

Promote Your Page

After your page has been approved by Compliance, start promoting it through your website and in your email signature with MailChimp or Constant Contact. Then you can begin inviting clients to "like" your page: go to your page, click on the three dots to the right of your background photo, and select "Invite Friends." Once someone has liked your page, they will see all of your updates in their newsfeed.

Now that you're up and running, you can begin posting your blog posts, videos, and updates to your business page to get more exposure. Then you can start running ads to get more people to like your page, register for an event you're planning, and drive traffic to your website. Be sure to "boost" each new article or video for $5 to triple the number of people who see the post.

Why You Should Invite Your Facebook Friends to Like Your Business Page

Here are a few key benefits of inviting personal Facebook friends to like your business page:

First and foremost, people who like your page will see your updates and the content you share, so they'll be more aware of what you do and how you can help. This could spell more referrals from them in the future.

Second, once someone has liked your page, Facebook will automatically recommend your page to their friends. Your clients' friends will see that they have liked your page and be able to like it themselves.

Facebook also shows your posts to people who are demographically similar to those who have liked your page. This means that if fifty of your clients have liked your page, Facebook will use its magic to show your posts to others just like them – presumably your ideal future clients.

Finally, Facebook automatically creates an advertising audience for you comprised of "people who like your page and their friends." You can use this audience to grow your network with paid ads in the future.

For these reasons, you'll want to invite some of your personal Facebook friends to like your page. Which ones? Only people who represent your target demographic or who can refer business to you.

Why You Shouldn't Invite Everyone to Like Your Page

Don't invite everyone you know to like your page because it will confuse the algorithm and dilute your audience with people who don't fit your target demographic.

Say you live in Chicago but you went to school in Florida and have a lot of friends from college that live down south. Should you invite them? Not if they don't represent your ideal client and they're unlikely to refer business to you.

Your content is likely to get low engagement from that audience, which can hurt your content in the long run. The more relevant your page audience is, the more valuable your content will be to that audience and the more engagement it will get.

How to Invite Your Facebook Friends to Like Your Business Page

[**NOTE:** Not all compliance departments allow you to invite your friends to like your business page, so check with your compliance team first to be safe.] First, go to your Facebook Business Page by searching the business name in the Facebook Search bar (or go to your custom page URL if you know it).

Next, click "Invite your friends to like this Page" in the right-hand column.

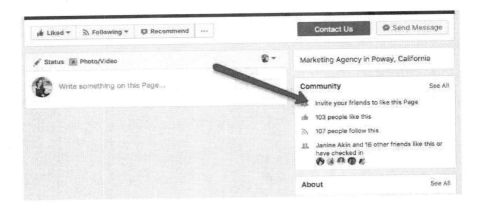

Then, in the pop-up window, customize the invitation message you would like your friends to receive. I recommend something like this:

Hi, I'm inviting you to like my business page so you can see the photos and helpful content we share. Thank you for supporting our firm!

Finally, select which friends you'd like to invite, and then click "Send Invites." (If a person's image has been grayed out, that means you've already invited them to like the page and they haven't responded yet.)

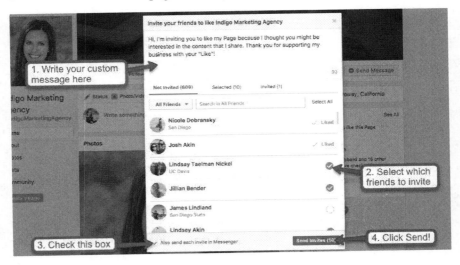

Your friends will receive a notification that they've been invited to like your page. Typically, we see 30–50 percent of recipients accept.

Email Asking Clients to Like Your Page

This step is obvious, but most advisors haven't done it. I recommend sending an email to let your clients know that your business is live on Facebook and asking them to like the page. Share a few recent photos or interesting posts from your page to let them know what they're missing.

Post Engaging Content and Boost to Your Target Audience

The best way to get people to like your page is to boost content that is interesting or valuable to them. My favorite way to do this on Facebook is with engaging infographics; one recent post got more than 1,000 clicks from Facebook the day it was posted.

Share Photos and Tag People

Truly successful Facebook Business Pages use photos from events and advisors' personal lives to engage their audience. Facebook is all about photos and videos, so if you're serious about Facebook, you'll want to regularly post real photos of you and your team. Tagging your clients and friends in the photos will show the posts to their friends.

Promote Your Page with Paid Ads

You can promote your page to get more likes. Use stringent audience parameters so you're only paying for likes from potential clients. Too many irrelevant page likes will throw off the Facebook algorithm and hurt you in the long run.

Try Facebook Pixels to Retarget Website Visitors

Digital advertising gets savvier every day. With Facebook Pixels, you can ensure your Facebook ads show up in the feeds only of people who have visited your website or even a certain page of your site. This is one of the most cost-effective ways to advertise because there's a good chance that someone who's visited your website will want to like to your Facebook page.

For example, I could show an ad about my Monthly Marketing Package only to people who have read a related blog post on my site recently. This will increase my ad's conversion rate, since I know the viewers are interested in the topic.

To take advantage of Pixels, there is some upfront work you have to do, including adding a code on your website and linking it with your Facebook Business Page. However, it doesn't take long, and after you've done it once, you're set.

Boost Your Posts

Boosting your posts is another inexpensive advertising option that can increase your Facebook likes and help you reach more people. For example, you could boost a post about your upcoming Social Security event to people in your neighborhood who are 65+ years old.

You can target by basic demographics, such as age range, location, and gender, as well as more specific fields, such as interests, employer, and job title. For this advertising option, I recommend boosting posts that link to a blog post on your website that covers a highly topical financial concern to grab viewers' attention.

Facebook ads are an inexpensive way for advisors to make contact with prospects they don't already know. The downside is that the ads are some- times poorly targeted, resulting in plenty of "junk" traffic. To reach people within your niche, you'll need to narrow the audience for your Facebook ads to focus on qualified prospects. Here are three clever ways to make sure you're advertising to the people who matter most to your firm:

1. Think About Your Competition

If you have a direct competitor in your town, you probably share potential customers. One easy way to find prospects is to use Facebook ads to target people that are interested in your competitor's pages or posts.

Search for the name of your competitor under "Interests > Additional Interests" when you're creating your advertising audience. People who have liked your competitor's page or clicked on *their* content will now see *your* ad.

2. Create a Lookalike Audience

Facebook has so much information on its users that it can "clone" them for advertising purposes. By using a "lookalike" audience, you can show your ad to people who are demographically similar to your existing clients.

You can create a lookalike audience by integrating your MailChimp account directly with Facebook, or simply by uploading a list of email addresses. Facebook reviews the information of the users you've selected and creates an audience that "matches" them.

3. Add a Link to Your Email Signature and Website

In your email signature, add a link to your Facebook page beneath your name. This is one of the easiest yet most effective ways to let people know about your Facebook page and encourage more likes.

Don't forget to also include a link to your Facebook on your website. Most website providers make it easy to feature the Facebook icon in your masthead or footer. When visitors click on the icon, it takes them to your Facebook page, where they can follow your business.

Facebook is a powerful tool for building your brand and getting in front of your network. Consumers today expect businesses to have an active and engaged business page showcasing their culture, so now is the time to get your page up and running.

Step 3: Set Up and Optimize Your Twitter Profile

While Facebook and LinkedIn might be the first social media platforms to come to mind for financial advisors, Twitter is also a valuable resource to take your business presence to the next level by showcasing your brand and services and increasing your exposure.

We all know what Twitter is today, thanks to Donald Trump. But what makes it different? Twitter is a unique social media platform in that it limits its users to 140-character tweets. These concise messages appear on your profile, which also showcases your photo, logo, bio, and link to your website. Anyone who visits your profile can see how many tweets you have posted, the number of followers you have, your recent tweets, and retweets and shares from others.

As part of our Referral Marketing Package, we create and optimize all of your social media profiles for you. Let me share our helpful checklist for setting up and optimizing your Twitter profile:

1. "Update Profile Picture" with your current logo. Make sure to use a square image file so it appears correctly, about 800 × 800 px for good image clarity.

2. "Update Cover Image." Make sure the image is at least 1500 × 500 px.

3. Click "Edit Profile."

4. Update your bio with a short version of your company description or mission statement.

5. Add your location.

6. Add your website link.

7. Choose a custom theme color to match your logo. If you don't know your exact color code, use a color grabber such as https://www.canva.com/color-palette/.

8. Click "Save Changes."

9. If you are just setting up this account and you'd like to change your profile URL (not recommended for established accounts):

   • Click your profile photo (logo) in the top right and select "Settings and Privacy."

   • Enter your new, desired username. You may need to adjust if it is unavailable. (Tip: Use common abbreviations if the name is unavailable, such as "Wlth," "Adv," or "Fin.")

   • Click "Save Changes" at the bottom of the screen and enter your Twitter password to confirm.

10. Revisit this process annually to make sure your images and bio are up to date.

Step 4: Join NAPFA

Have you considered joining NAPFA, the National Association of Personal Financial Advisors? Many of the most successful advisors I work with belong to NAPFA. They receive qualified leads through their membership and enjoy the networking and conferences that the association provides. In fact, one advisor receives upwards of 30 referrals per month from NAPFA, his main source of new clients. If you haven't thought about joining NAPFA, now may be a good time to consider the benefits.

What Is NAPFA?

NAPFA is a professional association of fee-only financial advisors. Investors can search napfa.org to find a registered fee-only advisor in their area. It was founded in 1983 by a group of advisors who wanted to provide financial advice without commissions. The association requires that all members sign and renew a Fiduciary Oath annually and subscribe to their Code of Ethics. They provide education, networking, and marketing support to their 3,000 members.

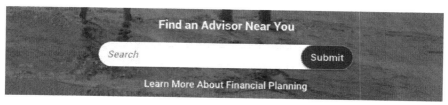

Benefits of NAPFA Membership

One important benefit NAPFA offers members is the referral of leads who are seeking a fee-only advisor. Member Ben Gurwitz explains, "In my experience, prospects who are seeking a fee-only planner gravitate to NAPFA and then to our website through the affiliated fee-only network. After realizing that we were getting dozens of referrals each month to our website from NAPFA's Fee-Only Network, we completely redesigned our site to speak to those visitors. In our city, there is a small list of fee-only advisors and we really benefit from the referrals."

Another advisor member explained, "The 'find an advisor' feature is the single largest source of new clients for me. Most of my clients found me by going to the NAPFA website after hearing about it on the Clark Howard show or from magazines and consumer-oriented news media. Almost everyone I meet with mentions something related to NAPFA."

Some advisors see NAPFA as a way to stand out from the crowd, like Debbie Gallant of Gallant Financial Planning. "I am a huge fan of NAPFA and I feel that I wave the flag for the organization's goals and requirements of being fee only and a fiduciary who also offers comprehensive planning services to clients."

Gallant shares, "The most important benefit of NAPFA is a set of ethics and professional parameters under which I offer my services to clients. Second is a fantastic community of like-minded professionals who truly are looking out for their clients. And the community that I have found through NAPFA is a warm and sharing group of colleagues who share their insights and experience in running their own practices with each other."

Of course, not everyone who searches for an advisor on the NAPFA website is a qualified lead. Some prospects lack the financial resources to pay the advisor's fee. For this reason, it's important for members to have an account minimum or a way of screening out unqualified prospects. Some members offer advice at no charge as part of their firm's community service.

Who Can Join?

NAPFA isn't for everyone, since you have to be a fee-only advisor and hold your CFP® designation. You also have to complete 60 hours of continuing education every 2 years and provide comprehensive financial planning services. If you fit these requirements, it may make sense for you to apply for membership.

To join NAPFA, advisors must pay a one-time $150 fee for new members as well as the annual dues of $665. A variety of membership levels for students, registered advisors, and retired members are listed on their site. Several advisors I spoke with felt that the benefits far outweigh the cost of membership. Debbie Gallant explains, "The referrals that I receive from the website more than adequately pay for the membership I pay each year. I can't think of many costs that I would not cut first before I would give up my membership."

To apply to become a NAPFA member, create an account and begin the application process on napfa.org. If you have any questions, contact membership@napfa.org.

CHAPTER 8

Warm Up Prospects with Webinars

WHAT IF EVERY visitor to your website spent 30 minutes with you to understand your background, what makes your firm different, and how you can help them? How would that impact your lead conversion rate? This is where webinar marketing lends a hand.

Most of the advisors I work with have a rock-solid value proposition that converts at 70–90 percent when they actually get a chance to sit down with a prospect. The problem is that their value propositions tend to be complex and tough to explain through text on a website.

This is where webinars can revolutionize a financial advisor's marketing. Webinars can quadruple your conversion rate when compared with email marketing. And today's technology makes webinars easier than ever to create.

I'm passionate about webinar marketing as the next frontier for advisors for a few reasons:

1. They're an Inexpensive Alternative to Seminars

We know that seminars are an effective marketing tool because so many advisors have used them to build their business in the past. But when you consider costs for the location, food, parking, and other expenses, they can be prohibitive. A webinar provides many of the benefits of a seminar, without the high costs.

2. They Make Complex Topics More Palatable

Whether you plan to educate employees of a company about the details of their pension plan or teach pre-retirees about strategies for claiming Social Security, you know that financial planning topics can be dry and confusing. Webinars make complex ideas easier to understand and more engaging.

3. You Can Use Them for Client Education

Top advisors use webinars to educate clients about market changes or keep them up to date on firm news and events. Webinars are a great way to help clients feel in the know without having to meet with each of them regularly one-on-one.

4. They Are Scalable for Small or Large Audiences

Unlike seminars, webinars have the same low cost whether you're running one for 50 or 500 prospects. Once you have put in the time and energy to create a webinar, you can share it with as many prospects as you can find.

5. They Feature a Call to Action

The goal of a prospecting webinar is to help the viewer understand a problem and its solution, and then urge them to take action. At the end of the webinar you can offer a free second opinion, introductory phone call, or insurance policy audit – whichever next step is appropriate for the viewer to take.

6. They Allow You to Capture the Email Addresses of Attendees

Even if webinar attendees do not take action after they sign up to view the presentation, you will have their email address. As you grow your email list and nurture your subscribers over time, more of them will eventually take action and do business with you.

7. They Have Conversion Rates of 20–40 Percent (vs. 2–5 Percent for Email)

Depending on your call to action, webinar conversion rates can be as high as 40 percent. Because viewers have invested their time and get so much information from a webinar presentation, they're much more likely to take the next step than someone who only reads an email.

8. They Can Be Used in Perpetuity

Once you have created a webinar and got it approved by Compliance, you can use it indefinitely to turn website visits into prospect appointments. I recommend creating a webinar for each important niche you serve.

Technologies You Need to Get Started

I'll be honest, DIYing a webinar is a lot of work. But if you're fairly tech-savvy and ready to put in 8–12 hours of effort, a webinar can be a powerful investment in your marketing. Here are my recommendations for eight technologies and services you will need to create your first webinar:

1. PowerPoint

The first step in creating your webinar is writing your presentation. There are a variety of presentation technologies out there, such as Prezi and Keynote, but I recommend using good old PowerPoint, even if you're on a Mac. Because PowerPoint is so widely used, you'll be able to have a graphics expert design the slides and send them back to you in an editable format.

2. Upwork.com

To turn your slides from text-only bullet points into a beautiful presentation in your firm's branding and color scheme, you'll want to work with a great graphic designer. I recommend finding one on Upwork.com, a freelance hiring website. Search for "PowerPoint designer" and make sure whoever you choose has five-star reviews. Plan to spend at least $5 per slide to get your project designed well.

3. A Good Camera (Optional)

It's not necessary, but if you want to be on screen during your webinar, you'll need a good camera to film yourself. There are a few options that will work well. Try using your iPhone to capture a landscape video. Or, if you have a MacBook, the built-in camera is fantastic. Want to go big? The Canon G7X is the best camera on the market for this type of recording. Just keep in mind that you'll need a memory card, tripod, and other accessories for a luxury camera setup.

4. A Great Microphone

Whether you plan to record video of yourself or simply do a voiceover of your slides, you'll need high-quality audio for your webinar. A USB microphone that plugs directly into your computer is your best bet. The Blue Yeti is the top-rated microphone for podcasting and is available on Amazon for about $130. It takes a little bit of work to learn how to use this microphone; make sure it's in Cardioid mode, sitting straight up and down, and that you speak directly toward the logo.

You should also consider using a pop filter to screen out harsh sounds and a shock mount to keep vibrations at bay. Another handy tool is a mobile sound booth, which is a noise-absorbing shield that goes around your microphone so it picks up only your voice.

5. Screen Recording Software

Once you have your PowerPoint designed and approved by Compliance, it's time to record your webinar. If you have a Mac, QuickTime will already be installed, so you can just click to "Start New Screen Recording." For Windows PCs, try SoapBox from Wistia, which makes it really easy to record from your built-in webcam then switch to recording your screen with audio. Another good option for Windows using GoToMeeting and recording the session.

6. Video Hosting

Once you've recorded your webinar and gotten the final version approved by Compliance, you'll need to host it somewhere on the Internet. I use Wistia, which is free for your first three videos. I find that it looks less cluttered and more professional than Vimeo or YouTube.

7. Webinar Automation Software

They key to an effective marketing webinar is setting it up to run on auto-pilot so that you can use it forever. Webinar automation software takes care of such things as the registration page, reminder emails, a countdown clock, and playing the webinar at the time someone signed up to watch it. Then you can customize follow-up and replay emails. I use EasyWebinar, which is $497 per year.

8. Email Marketing Software

After a prospect watches your webinar, you'll want to persuade them to take the next step with you. By scheduling follow-up emails in the days and weeks after the webinar, you can maximize your conversion rate. I recommend MailChimp to set up a four-email workflow that runs automatically. It's free for fewer than 2,000 contacts.

How to Create Your First Webinar

Webinars are an incredibly powerful marketing tool, but getting started on your first one can be overwhelming. Try to avoid perfectionism: remember that you can always update your webinar later. The most important thing is to get up and running so you can gather feedback and improve. Follow these steps to create your first webinar:

Step 1: Select Your Topic

The topic of your webinar is critically important. It's worthwhile to do some research or run some tests when you're deciding what to cover for your first webinar. You'll want to focus on an urgent problem facing a specific group of people.

The best webinars are laser-focused and give away a ton of specific value. Don't be tempted to go too broad here, or your webinar will blend into all of the noise out there. Top-performing webinars my clients have done include:

- *How Intel Employees Can Prepare for the Next Round of Layoffs*
- *What Should Bristol-Myers Squibb Employees Do about the Pension Buyout?*
- *How Divorced and Widowed Women Can Maximize Their Social Security Benefits*
- *How Doctors Can Catch Up for Retirement in a Hurry*

Here are some ways to decide what's the best fit for your firm;

Check Out Your Google Analytics

If you have Google Analytics set up for your website, it's easy to see which pages are the most popular. Just go to "Behavior," then "Overview" to see your top ten pages. Make sure you change the date range to the last year or so to capture data for a wide range of visitors.

My recent post on "How to Get New Clients During a Market Decline" has the most views on my website. This is a good indication that a webinar on how to use market volatility in your marketing strategy would be alluring to my visitors.

Test Ideas Using Facebook Ads

Whenever I plan a new webinar, I test out the topic and title using Facebook ads. It's easy to set up an ad that goes to my main webinar library and run it with different titles of topics I might want to cover. Then I compare results and go with the lowest cost per click, which indicates which title the largest number of people clicked on.

Ask Your Clients

You can do a quick survey of your clients to find out what they'd most like you to cover in a webinar. Using Google Forms or Survey Monkey, ask your clients to select from among three to five options. When I did this for my email list, the feedback was overwhelming that advisors wanted me to do a webinar on Facebook ads next. If you don't want to be so formal, simply ask a few trusted clients for their feedback.

Step 2: Name Your Webinar

Like the topic, the title of your webinar is really important. I've seen great webinars fail because the title was boring. Put on your marketing hat and name your webinar something exciting. You can test out titles to see which one performs best. Here are some examples of great webinar titles:

- *Social Security: The Choice of a Lifetime*
- *The Truth about Your Intel Benefits Package*
- *Six Unexpected Risks to Your Retirement*
- *Demystifying the Bristol-Myers Squibb Pension Plan Closure*

Titles that include "the truth," "the biggest mistakes," or "demystifying" do really well.

Step 3: Create Your Presentation

Once you've selected a topic, it's time to map out your presentation. At Indigo Marketing Agency, we always use the same formula, which is based on research by NASA. The smart folks at NASA scientifically proved that presentations around 17–20 minutes long are ideal for viewers to retain information. This translates to about eighteen slides.

While you're mapping out your presentation, you'll just need slides with text. Don't worry about design, fonts, or formatting at this point. If you have relevant graphics, you can include them, but don't spend energy on the design of your presentation. I typically open up a blank presentation and simply add one short sentence to each slide.

Slide 1: Title and Subtitle

Ex: *What Should You Do About the Bristol-Myers Squibb Pension Buyout?*

How BMS Employees Can Plan to Maximize Their Benefits

Slide 2: Your Credentials

This slide should include your background, education, licenses, and firm affiliation. This answers the question "Why am I uniquely suited to teach this course?"

Ex: *I've been working with BMS employees for two decades and am personally familiar with the pension plan.*

Slide 3: Your Mission

This slide should capture why you became a financial advisor and why you're passionate about it. Until people understand what motivates you, they can't begin to trust you.

Ex: *My wife works at BMS and I understand how confused and worried employees are about their benefits. I'm here to help you feel confident about selecting the best option for you so you can get back to work.*

Slide 4: About Them

This is your opportunity to communicate how well you understand the viewer. Relate to the challenges facing them, their background, why they face urgency now, and their fears.

Ex: *You've likely worked at BMS for decades and always thought the pension plan would be there for you. Now it's closing and you face a critical decision that you must make within 90 days.*

Slide 5: The Urgent Problem

Here you'll review the important choice they'll have to make – whether that's retirement planning, Social Security, or financial planning – and how it will impact them.

Ex: *This is your only chance to choose a lump-sum payout to receive cash for your pension benefits. This represents an incredible opportunity, but with considerable risk. It's critical to choose the best option for your specific situation, and if you do take the lump-sum option, invest the money in line with your risk tolerance.*

Slides 6–14: The Details

Here's where you'll cover the meat of the presentation and your expertise on the topic.

Ex: *The history of the pension plan, the options available, potential scenarios, critical points to consider, etc.*

Slide 15: Emotional Confrontation

This is the key slide of your presentation. Confront the viewer with an uncomfortable emotional reality if they fail to take action.

Ex: *If you do not take the lump-sum payout option, you will likely never get another opportunity to access your retirement benefits and invest them in a way that aligns with your best interests.*

This could leave you with a drastically reduced standard of living in retirement.

Slide 16: A Powerful Solution

Here's where you offer an easy action for them to take to alleviate the emotional discomfort you caused in the last slide.

Ex: *Schedule your complimentary one-on-one consultation with our team and we'll review your specific situation, answer your questions, and provide recommendations to maximize your pension benefits.*

Slide 17: Call to Action

Urge viewers to take action now by scheduling a call, signing up for a meeting, or filling out a "Get Started Now" form.

> Ex: *Click below to schedule your meeting today. Remember, you only have 90 days to choose your payout option, so reserve your space now to make sure you are fully informed and confident in your decision.*

Slide 18: How to Learn More

This slide is for people who are not ready to make the big jump and complete your call to action. Give them a way to learn more about the topic and keep in touch with you.

> Ex: *Download our free report on how to make the most of your pension plan options and join our newsletter for up-to-the-minute updates and news.*

Step 4: Design Your Presentation

We have an amazing PowerPoint graphic designer on our team who creates beautiful presentations for our clients. A trained designer will ensure each slide is properly branded, easy to read, and consistent.

To get your presentation designed on your own, I recommend using Upwork.com and searching for "PowerPoint designer." Take a look at their reviews, samples of their work, and their rate. Aim to pay $100–200 to have your presentation designed.

Make sure you give the designer the following:

- Your logo
- Your headshot
- Your branding color scheme
- Any graphs or charts
- A photography theme (beaches, golf, business owners, etc.)

Once you get your designed presentation back, send it through Compliance. Make any required changes, and then you're ready to record.

Step 5: Record Your Webinar

This is the point where most advisors get stuck. You've already done 80 percent of the work, but many people get paralyzed by perfectionism and never record their webinar.

My best advice to overcome this is to schedule a time on your calendar to make the recording and commit to yourself to get it done. Then, the day before you plan to record, do a complete run-through of your presentation.

When the time comes to record, accept no excuses and record as if it were live. You can always update your recording later, but it is critical to get your first webinar out and start collecting feedback to make it better.

Step 6: Automate Your Webinar

I recommend running automated webinars, for a few reasons:

- You can get your full webinar approved by Compliance in advance
- There is no risk of technical difficulties
- People still think automated webinars are live
- Data shows that twice as many people watch an automated webinar as a live one, since about half of them watch the replay

My favorite webinar automation tool is EasyWebinar. It's pretty robust and can be overwhelming, so if you're not tech-savvy, you'll want to outsource this piece of the puzzle. Our team can help upload and automate your webinar for you – a service that includes:

- Uploading your logo and headshot
- Creating your presenter bio section
- Creating your registration page
- Configuring the dates and times your webinar will be available
- Creating automatic reminders to go out one day and one hour before it starts
- Adding your "offer" pop-up and countdown timer to get people to take action
- Adding your links, notes, and offer to the event page

- Adding the presentation video to the event page
- Adding an invitation video to the registration page

Once you've automated your webinar, sign up to watch it and make sure everything is configured properly.

Step 7: Promote Your Webinar

Now that your webinar is up and running and you have a registration page to share, it's time to promote your webinar. You worked hard to create a valuable presentation, so don't be shy about inviting everyone you know to watch.

Invite Your Network by Email

First, I recommend emailing out several promotional emails to your list. This communication should include a short video inviting them to attend the webinar and explaining what you'll cover and why it's so important. Schedule at least four emails inviting them to watch:

1. Save the Date for Our Upcoming Webinar
2. Register Now for Our Webinar
3. Last Chance to Register for Our Webinar
4. Watch the Replay of Our Webinar

Leverage LinkedIn

Especially for employer-specific webinars, LinkedIn is the way to get your presentation in front of people you don't already know. Have your assistant send messages to everyone who fits your target demographic inviting them to attend. If you don't hear back, send a follow-up message with a link to the replay. You can even use an automated LinkedIn tool to invite people in bulk.

Consider Facebook Ads

If your target audience isn't on LinkedIn but you still want to get in front of people you don't already know, Facebook ads could be an option. You can create ads to target people by location, age, gender, and interests. For example, you could target friends of people who have liked your page, presuming that the ads would be displayed to your clients' friends. Get creative with your Facebook ads to target your ideal prospects.

Share with Referral Partners

The best way to get your webinar in front of more qualified prospects is to ask referral partners to share it with their clients. If you work with a lawyer, CPA, or other professional who serves the same demographic, they may agree to invite their clients to attend your webinar as a value-add for people in their network.

Step 8: Follow Up to Convert Viewers

Only a small percentage of webinar viewers will take action on the day they watch your webinar. In fact, the average time between when someone views a webinar and when they become a client is about 1 year.

This means that you need to regularly follow up with viewers to make sure you're top of mind when they finally get around to making a move. I recommend a follow-up series of four-to-six emails inviting them to take action. Here are some examples of top-performing follow-up email automations:

1. Thanks for Watching Our Webinar—What Did You Think?
2. Do You Have Questions about Your Specific Situation?
3. Schedule Your Free One-on-One Consultation Today
4. Why I Became a Financial Advisor
5. What We Do & How We Can Help
6. Do You Know Someone Who Needs Our Help?
7. Did You Know You Can Make an Appointment Online?
8. Let's Get Coffee and Get to Know Each Other

Once your email series has completed, add all the webinar viewers to your regular email list so they'll see your updates. You can also have your assistant connect with them on LinkedIn so they'll see your posts and be able to get in touch with you there.

I know this all may seem like a lot of work, but webinars are incredibly powerful. When you consider setting up an automated webinar or hosting a dinner seminar, the costs and work involved don't compare.

For a seminar, you have to do all the work to prepare and give a presentation – and pay for everyone's dinner. A webinar will run forever, twenty-four hours a day.

You can continue to promote your webinar to get more viewers, which will grow your email list and put new appointments on your calendar. You can use the webinar as a foot in the door with cold leads or send it as a follow-up after you meet with prospects.

Add it to the end of each blog post or email that you send. Share it on your social media profiles so people can watch to learn more about you. Add it front and center to your website's homepage to provide a dynamic way to introduce yourself to new people. Investing in your first webinar can go a long way in supporting the rest of your marketing strategy and growing your firm now and into the future.

CHAPTER 9

Getting in front of People You Don't Already Know

ONCE YOU HAVE a great website and you're constantly driving new referrals, the last frontier for growing your business is getting in front of people you do not already know. Of course, these prospects are more difficult to find and harder to close, but once you do, they can refer you to their untapped network.

To get you in front of new people in your target demographic, we use two strategies in our Lead Generation Package:

LinkedIn Campaigns

First, we target the people you'd like to connect with using LinkedIn's advanced search parameters. Criteria could include people in a certain industry, people with a certain job title, or employees of a certain company.

We send 450 outbound connection requests on your behalf each month. (You can use a virtual assistant or a third-party tool such as LinkedHub to accomplish this yourself.) We find that 20–30 percent of people accept your connection request, which grows your network and allows them to see your posts in the future.

Once someone accepts your request and becomes a new connection, we send a follow-up message on your behalf with relevant information and the opportunity to schedule a phone call if they need your help.

Here's an example:

Hi John,

Thanks for connecting. I specialize in helping ADP employees create a plan to retire on time here in New Jersey. I recently wrote a report about how to maximize your ADP benefits package that you can download here.

If you have questions about your own retirement account, please schedule a 15-minute phone call here.

Best,

Tom

Facebook Ads

Second, we use Facebook ads to get in front of new people that fit your target demographic. The parameters include age, gender, location, interests, hobbies, and employer.

We test up to twenty variations of ads until we get one that is less than $1.00 per click. (The average Facebook ad is $1.73 per click, so getting to $1.00 is a big achievement.)

When someone clicks on your ad, they go to a landing page on your website where they're encouraged to watch a video, download a report, or schedule a phone call. They're added to your email list and receive four follow-up emails encouraging them to take the next step with you. We aim for a website conversion rate of at least 10 percent.

If you're not an expert in Facebook ads, I encourage you to hire someone who knows what they're doing. The process can be overwhelmingly technical.

The Results

With our Lead Generation Package, you can expect five to ten new leads each month. Depending on your close rate, this typically translates to between one and four new clients each month.

A great marketing plan must have a strategy both to nurture your referral pipeline by staying top-of-mind and to get in front of new people as a specialist with a piece of content that "hooks" them. By building a marketing engine to get in front of new leads, you not only grow your business by adding clients, but greatly increase your potential for more referrals.

CHAPTER 10

How to Build a Career (and Life) That You Love

MAYBE IT'S BECAUSE most advisors have the heart of a salesperson that I rarely find an advisor who is not trying to grow their business. Whatever the assets under management or number of clients advisors currently serve, most are always striving to build something bigger.

In working with hundreds of advisors, I have identified four common traits of advisors who are growing their practices year after year that are absent in advisors who are losing ground.

1. They Believe in Their Value

You can tell right away when you are talking to an advisor who honestly believes that they give their clients more in value than they take in compensation. Their worldview is that of abundance, and they know that if they lose a client, there are plenty other folks out there who would benefit from their services.

They say things like "I only take on new clients I can help" or "I can only serve 100 families, so I choose carefully when working with someone new." These advisors work with optimism in the referral process and a calm confidence in their business. Their concerns typically surround business efficiencies and finding referrals to their ideal clients. Believing in their value helps them attract new clients and close business when the client is a good fit.

2. They Invest in Technology and Marketing

I have found that all advisors who are growing their business invest significantly in technology and marketing. Of the advisors I have worked with who were increasing AUM, over half used Redtail CRM, eMoney, and FMG Suite.

The correlation makes me wonder about causation. Did they grow their business because of their technology? Or are they able to invest because their revenue is consistently climbing? I suspect they are growing their business because they have a systematic and disciplined approach to investing in technology and marketing.

Some cite numbers, such as 3 percent of revenue goes back into marketing efforts. These investments result in more efficient and more productive business models and make finding new clients easy. You would never attempt to run a marathon without food and water, yet trying to grow your business without feeding your technology and marketing engines ends in the same miserable, frustrating, and painful result.

3. They Are Comfortable with "Good Enough"

The greatest threat to effective marketing is perfectionism. I have seen so many advisors never launch their website because they can't get comfortable with each word on each page. They fail to see the credibility hit they take by not having a website at all.

The same is true for perfectionists when it comes to blogging. In the attempt to increase accuracy, advisors conduct painful rounds of edits to their blog posts, decreasing their posting frequency and killing their enjoyment of the process. What they don't realize is that most readers don't care about detailed facts and figures.

People read your blog because they want your expertise and opinion. Someone looking for basic facts will go to Wikipedia, not your blog. Blogs are a place to share ideas, a living, breathing conversation, not a scientific journal. The goal is to deliver insightful ideas with a personal touch.

Advisors who are growing their business stick to a schedule and get their content out no matter what. The most successful advisors recognize the power of consistent marketing and make arrangements so it happens on a regular basis.

4. They Think about the Client Experience

I love it when I am talking to an advisor and they use language that describes how their clients actually experience the services, marketing, and communication from their firm. They say things like "When my clients sit down at their computer, they have thirty or so marketing emails. I want ours to feel different."

This shows that they have taken the time and effort to visualize how their clients spend their day and are sensitive to their circumstances. How do they feel when they receive an email from the advisor? Is the firm's technology easy for them to use? Does it add value for them?

Most advisors long for continued, sustainable growth year over year. They want to serve more clients, grow their firm, and create a lasting legacy. At the same time, they don't want service levels for existing clients to suffer and they don't want to work more hours.

I believe that the trick to accomplishing this lies in embracing technologies and efficiencies in client service and marketing, then changing the mindset of your marketing from "advertising" to "helping people find you when they need you most."

There is no substitute for pondering what your clients value and how to make their lives easier. If you are disciplined with your marketing efforts, you will consistently reach clients you can help and serve more of them each year.

What Do You Really Want from Your Career (and Your Life)?

Success can be a mysterious thing, and there's no clear formula for building a thriving financial advisory practice. I'm always looking for factors that make the difference between a struggling financial advisor and a successful one. But those factors aren't always easy to see.

Some of my advisors work tirelessly through their days and nights; others golf in the afternoons and are never in the office on a Friday. Some are interested in their marketing, and others have no idea how it works. Some still do cold-calling and seminars, while others never lift a finger to grow their business.

But all the differences aside, I noticed a while back that my three most successful advisor clients (who didn't know each other) have three things in common:

1. They are exceptionally kind
2. They're fervently passionate about what they do
3. They're incredibly positive people

Is this a coincidence? I don't think so. At the risk of sounding kooky, I fully believe that you attract into your life what you put out into the universe in the form of thoughts. Positive people have been proven to be more successful in life and in business. It's important to be positive and get clear about what you want from your business.

Get Clear on What You Want and Share It

Have you ever had the experience of putting an idea out into the ether and having it materialize for you? This happened to me last week. I was telling my husband that I would love to be able to give back through my business school (the Rady School of Management at UC San Diego) by helping other alumni start their own business. That's what I'm passionate about and what I would love the opportunity to do. But I wasn't sure how.

The next day, I got a call from an old classmate. He had been selected to be the president of the alumni association. He was calling to see whether I would be interested in running the alumni association entrepreneurship group. Bingo!

I see similar things happen all the time for my clients and my friends. Once you get clear about what you want, the opportunity you're looking for will present itself.

Do You Love What You Do?

But what if you're not excited about growing your firm? Then you need to change what you're doing.

Take a step back and get crystal clear on what you want out of life. As you know by now, your career as a financial advisor will ultimately also become your life and your identity. To find happiness in both, you need to be doing something you find enjoyable, important, and valuable.

So many advisors out there are chasing clients they think will build a great business. If you try to work with engineers because they're high earners but you hate working with engineers, please stop! If you're going for high-net-worth clients to grow your AUM but they make your life miserable, it's time to do some soul searching.

I worked with one advisor who said he only takes on new clients who are "hard workers and really nice people." He made a point of having everyone on his team "fire" one client per year who didn't fit that description. Not coincidentally, he is one of the most successful advisors in the country. I was impressed that he had found a way to characterize the clients that made his job enjoyable each day.

When you figure out your true mission, it's easy and fun to share that with others. You'll find yourself happy to talk about your passion with anyone, instead of drained after making a sales pitch. The key to successful marketing is deeply intertwined with finding a passion that you are eager to share with the world.

So what does that mean for you? What is your passion? Are you really excited to spend your life helping people lower the risk in their 401(k)? Or is there something better out there for you?

Here are the missions of some advisors who are really passionate about what they do:

- *I help divorced women create a plan for retirement that they can look forward to.*

- *I help business owners pass their firm to their children and retire with true wealth.*

- *I help world travelers manage their finances in a way that brings them freedom.*

What is the best gift that you bring your clients? What is the best use of your talents? What do you really love to do? When people ask you what you do, what do you wish you could say?

Once you can find the answer that excites you the most, you're ready to grow your business and build a life and career you truly love. I wish you the best of luck for a happy and prosperous future!

Made in the USA
Middletown, DE
20 October 2022

13140563R00091